There You Have It!

Tales of a Wild Ride

MARY LYNN VAN LOON

iUniverse, Inc.
New York   Bloomington

There You Have It!
Tales of a Wild Ride

iUniverse books may be ordered through booksellers or by contacting:

iUniverse
1663 Liberty Drive
Bloomington, IN 47403
www.iuniverse.com
1-800-Authors (1-800-288-4677)

ISBN: 978-1-4502-3939-4 (pbk)
ISBN: 978-1-4502-3940-0 (ebk)

Printed in the United States of America

iUniverse rev. date: 8/4/10

Dedication

To all my children with love...

Acknowledgements

Warm thanks to Martha Loeffler whose encouragement inspired me, to the members of my writing group for their continuing support and for laughing at all the right places, to C. D. G. for assisting with the technical stuff, and to D. L. G. for coming up with a book cover.

CONTENTS

Preface xi
I'm from xiii

Livingston, California 1
What Can You Do with a Loaf of Bread 6
Look Mom! 9
There's Gold in Them Thar Hills 12

Whidbey Island 21
Prize Costume 23
Nature's Rhythm 28
Keepsies 41
On Our Way To Riches 45
The Game 52
Sex Education: 1939 Style 57
Louise's Revenge 59
The View from the Outhouse 64
My Secret 66
The Problem with Shoes 71

Crescent City Redwoods 75
Gone, but Not Forgotten 77
It's Only a Car 84

La Grange, California 91
Moving Up 93
Bittersweet Days 96

Modesto, California 105
The Light 107
Smile and the Whole World Smiles with You 113
Lovers 118
The Merger 124
Lunch at Carmen's! 131

Porterville, California 135
And Now--The Rest of the Story 138
Jack Frost and Other Real Life Heroes...................................... 141
Talking Dirty 144
Chopped Liver 145
Home Sweet….. 146

Riverbank, California 151
One of Life's Little Oops 153
I'll Never Forget You 156
A Time for Courage 159
Neighborhood Watch.. 162
Jumping to Conclusions.. 166
Haste Makes Waste 171
Incident at Deception Pass 174
Love At First Sight.. 177
Open Letter To Lena 179
Hello Reality 185

PREFACE

For many years, I talked about writing. Like thousands of others, I knew I had the great American novel just waiting to be put to paper. Always, too busy running my family and the world to sit down and get started, I avoided facing the truth. I was scared; I didn't know if I had the discipline or the ability to carry out my dream. So as long as I could use excuses such as work, volunteering full-time or not having a typewriter or computer, I felt I was safely off the hook. When all these self imposed roadblocks suddenly disappeared, I had the opportunity to attend a writing class and it was "put up or shut up" time.

The class is primarily for those who desired to write their memoirs, but others are welcome. When I began the class the idea of exposing myself was a major concern. I feared that some of my dark past was too shameful or embarrassing to share with others. I worried that if anyone knew the real me I would lose the respect that I have coveted most of my life. I was particularly concerned about what my children and grandchildren might make of some of my life adventures. Much of what is written is based on my actions in the past, which now embarrass me. I was anxious to get started, and was able, with the support of the instructor and encouragement of my fellow classmates, put my fears aside. I found that once I examined a memory, which had been hidden somewhere deep in my subconscious, and wrote it down, I could better understand the person I had been.

Surprisingly I found that I have a great sense of recall about things that happened fifty, sixty, even seventy-five years ago. In some situations I am unable to remember the entire dialogue, so using an author's prerogative I write my own. I write about what was once a painful happening and give it a little twist and finally laugh at myself. I wasn't sure if this would work, but when I read the essays, as part of class exercise, my peers reacted with delight and laughed with, not at me. Stepping to one side, I saw my life as a series of lessons learned shaping the person I am today. At long last I am able to rise above the hurt or embarrassment, and in doing so, I have "showed them" whoever "them" are.

Some family members, with whom I shared a story or two, remembered the incidents differently and felt compelled to correct my faulty recollection. I quickly put a stop to that, good intentions they may have been, and abolished one and all. "You can correct my spelling and punctuation, you may comment on the format, but leave my story line alone. These are my memories."

I have been fortunate to live a long and extremely eventful life, but I'm not through yet. I thought of calling this collection of essays "Memoirs of a Roller Coaster Journey." Thinking it over I decided that using "roller coaster" in the title implied loss of control or lack of choice, and is not the message I wish to send. In all things I believe there are choices, some are just better than others. For one reason or other I have not always made the right choice, but life has been good to me. Many times over the years I would find myself in a black hole thinking there was no way out due to my own actions, but then I would get another, and yet another, chance to get it right. It now appears that I have used the same philosophy in living that I use in driving. If I get lost or unable to find my destination, I do not panic, I just keep going and going and finally I'm where I'm supposed to be.

I find humor to be a gift that enables me to be creative and touch others deep within themselves. Laughter is a group activity and together it reminds us that we should not take ourselves too seriously. There is no record of anyone dying from embarrassment, even though I can think back when I thought I might. When I describe a social blunder or childhood slight, and my life has been full of them, you may recognize someone you once knew. You may be reminded of things that have happened in your own life, the twists and turns that have taken you by surprise, but now brings delight to your heart. Not everyone finds the same stories funny, as taste differs especially in matters of humor. Look for the laughs and cherish the pain. I hope you will find more than a few of my memories pleasing to your soul.

I'm from ...

I'm from wind swept prairie grass, which bred stoic men and women with gnarled hands, corncob pipes and sun kissed wrinkles by age thirty-five.

I'm from tear filled eyes as dirt covered the small coffin of a wee babe torn from her mother's breast. The Grim Reaper, an enemy to pioneer mothers, perched on her shoulder and grinned.

I'm from a country schoolhouse filled with inquisitive minds until the field's bounty over shadowed the pull of education. The need to fill the belly triumphed over the thirst for knowledge.

I'm from the determination of an orphan girl, born in frozen darkness and tossed by fate to the land of dreams and the welcome of "The Lady's" torch.

I'm from a lonely Canadian wanderlust, spiritual brother of timber wolves, who found a home in the Wyoming territory through the arms of the Orphaned Ice Queen.

I'm from a fairy tale written in golden promises, pledged by love and beauty, at Bridal Veil Falls, with Half Dome silently standing guard, soon vanished by reality.

I'm from a three-room shanty fashioned by my father's hammer tied to dusty streets and the crash of '29. As tumbleweeds became kites, hunger became my companion.

I'm from seeking the green grass promised just over the fence, leaving everything known and familiar, for a new beginning.

I'm from nature's paradise growing fins and seaweed for hair and running wild with deer and bobcats.

I'm from the Church of Christian Fellowship innocently witnessing evil, thinly cloaked by the holy word and under pretext of saving souls while the predator spun his evil.

Mary Lynn Van Loon

I'm from country roads with frogs croaking mating calls, squatting in rain fed ditches that guarded alder saplings and snow-covered cedars dwarfed by towering Douglas firs felled by the logger's axe.

I'm from an inner itch that never got scratched as I hurried into stormy adolescence wearing a victory bob, attending war bond drives and kissing young men as they marched to their death among the far-flung beaches of foreign shores.

I'm from the total sum of my fore-bearers and life experiences, my destiny determined by the wheel of chance. I'm terrified but ready, so watch out world, here I come!

Livingston, California

1927-1935

The Rug

May 1932

The rug was placed in the center of the room when we returned to class from recess. I pretended I didn't see it. I hated that rug! It was old, dull brown, with several worn areas where hundreds of kindergarten children had sprawled over the years. It wasn't the color, or the fact that it was old and worn, but what it signified for the four or five children that were banished to sit on it each day. What was their crime? It cost five cents for the morning snack for the week and they didn't have a nickel.

This particular morning I realized how much I truly hated being separate from the group and forced to sit on the rug. There were five of us on the rug. We sat, pretending that we didn't care, as our classmates enjoyed their milk and graham crackers. Sally, my playmate, always brought her nickel; her mother was a teacher. Today Sally was sitting next to the teacher, Mrs. Powers, and didn't look at me. I glanced over at the three boys and one other girl who were sharing the rug with me. It dawned on me that they were all from Mexican families. I was the only "white" child there. At home I was not allowed to cross the tracks and play with the kids who lived in the shacks near the packinghouses. Although it wasn't said in so many words, I knew we were better than they were. So how was it that I was here with Jose, Jorge, Manuel and Maria? In my daydreams I secretly believed I was a long lost princess and I was sure that when the teacher found out I'd be able to sit anywhere I wanted.

Returning to the classroom several days later, I noticed that today's milk had just been delivered. I counted fourteen little bottles of milk for those who had brought their money. Beside it sat a crate with empty bottles waiting to be picked up. *Whoa! What's this?* I asked myself. There was a bottle of last Friday's milk sitting in the crate with the empties. My devious mind recognized the opportunity, and without considering the consequences, I took the old bottle of milk and added it to the crate of milk delivered today. Now there were fifteen bottles of milk.

When it was time, we lucky ones all crowded to the table for our crackers and milk. Oh, it felt so good sitting here with the others! "Hands in your lap, everyone," said Mrs. Powers. "Today," she continued, "Jimmy will pass out the milk and straws. Glenda, will you please give everyone a napkin and two crackers?" I knew the ritual -- I'd watched it often enough from the rug.

While the crackers and milk were being passed out we all sang "We're all in our places," and I lifted my voice with the others, "With sunshiny faces."

"All right children, you may start."

From my lofty perch of the *rich and famous*, I looked down with indifference to the four or five classmates sitting forlornly on the wretched rug. As I took a long sip of cold milk a banging on the table interrupted my pleasure. Mrs. Powers demanded our attention. Next to a sniffling Sally, she stood holding an open bottle of milk for all to see. "This milk is spoiled,' announced Mrs. Powers, "How can that be? I know I ordered fourteen bottles of milk this morning and now I see fifteen children at the table. How can that be? And," she continued, "one of the bottles of milk is spoiled. Someone must have put a spoiled bottle from last Friday with the newly delivered milk. Who did this?"

We all looked around to see who the guilty party might be. I was not feeling too good about the turn of events. Surveying the faces at the table Mrs. Power's x-ray eyes lit on me. She had never seen me at the snack table before. "Mary, when we did the snack- count this morning, I don't remember you raising your hand." Looking at each face sitting around the table she asked, "Do any of you remember Mary raising her hand?"

I felt fourteen pairs of accusing eyes focused on me. A loud collective, "No," sealed my fate. Darn, trial by a jury of my peers and found guilty on all counts!

The crowning humiliation occurred as I tried to slink down to the rug where I obviously belonged. Mrs. Powers addressed me scornfully, "Never mind, Mary, you might as well finish. No one wants that milk after you've drunk most of it." I wondered if I would ever get off the rug and sit at the table again.

I took the long way home from school, trying to think up a good story about what happened today. I wasn't surprised when I saw my mother waiting for me when I finally got home. It was going to be a Mary Lynn afternoon. My name is Mary, but it was Mary Lynn when things got serious. Eventually, as my reputation for trouble spread, Mary Lynn evolved to Marilynn. This saved a lot of time for everyone.

Now was the hard part. My mother always wanted to know why I did the things I did, that got me in trouble. "Tell me what happened at school today Mary Lynn."

Eyes averted, I stammered, "I don't know."

"Is it true you took milk that belonged to Sally?" I thought about what she asked and realized that technically I didn't exactly take Sally's milk, she just got unlucky. I decided the whole thing was too complicated to try explaining. I didn't think my mother would want to hear about my being a princess. So I just started crying. I was good at crying; it sometimes helped when I was dealing with my father, but my mother was made of sterner stuff. "Young lady, I want you to sit right here and think about what you did today. You are to stay in that chair until you tell me what ever possessed you to do such a thing."

I tried to think what I could say about how I felt, banished to the rug while others sat at table. I just couldn't find the words. I went to bed early, but as usual I listened in on my parents talking after they thought I was asleep. I got kind of a sick feeling in the pit of my stomach hearing my mother cry. She told my father she didn't know how to explain to a five-year-old why some children had to sit on the floor and watch, while others drank cold milk and ate graham crackers. I could hear the back door slam as my father left the house without answering.

What Can You Do with a Loaf of Bread

May 1933

One particular spring day Sally in her pink organdy and me in my ruffled yellow dress were poking our way home from Sunday school. We chatted as six-year olds do, about nothing and every thing. The lesson that day was the story of Jesus feeding the multitude with only a couple fish and a loaf of bread. Sally said she didn't think one loaf of bread would feed more than ten people. I thought it would be more like about fifteen.

My mother had given me instructions to come straight home from church and not stop to play at Sally's house, as I normally liked to do. To reach our homes, from the church, we had to walk across the main street that was in downtown Livingston.

All this talk about Jesus feeding the poor led us to realize that we were hungry. As we walked passed Court's General Mercantile, we discussed getting something to eat from the store. Neither of us had any money, having given our pennies at the offering.

"My mom gets our food here. She just tells Mr. Court to write it down," I said feeling very grown-up. "She just tells him to put it on the tab."

Sally looked in the window at the jars of penny candy. "They won't let you do that, will they? You're not old enough." Even at six Sally was a born salesman.

"Oh sure, I do it all the time." I replied, stretching the truth as far as it would go. "Come on, I'll show you, it's real easy."

Sally wanted to get some candy bars. Even as young as I was, I realized that Mr. Court would not believe that my mother would send me to the store to buy candy. This was the middle of the depression years and candy was not a basic food item. We decided we would settle for a loaf of bread. As I entered the store, Sally, my partner in crime, lost her nerve and decided to stay out on the sidewalk. I didn't say it then, but I would never completely trust her again. However, I was determined to get the bread, so I plunged ahead.

I studied the selection of different breads and took one that looked familiar to the counter. Avoiding Mr. Court's look, I glanced around as if to see if there was anything else I was supposed to buy. "Put this on my mom's bill." I said with my heart in my throat.

"Did your mother send you to the store to buy this bread?" he wanted to know.

I was too scared to answer, so I just nodded my head. "Your mom never sent you here by yourself before, Mary. Are you sure she wanted you to buy this bread?"

I was ready to bolt and run out of the store, but couldn't decide if I should grab the bread or leave it. Finally I managed to get out a meek, "Yes, my mom wants this bread."

"Well, I guess it's alright, but I'll have to talk to her about it." Almost crying with relief I left the store the proud owner of a large loaf of white bread. Sally, once again eager to be my friend, caught up with me and together we walked along the sidewalk wondering what to do next. "Let me carry the bread, Mary. You're squashing it."

"OK, you can carry it for a while, but remember it's mine."

When we got to the library we sat on the steps and Sally started to open the end of the wrapping. The smell of fresh baked bread is like nothing else. Just then a small car pulled up next to the library and my mother stepped out onto the sidewalk. I could see my favorite uncle behind the steering wheel. He must have come for an unexpected visit.

Darn, I thought, *caught with the goods.*

The loaf of bread Sally was holding was suddenly thrust into my lap. "Here's your bread," she said, as she stood up. "I have to get home; my mother will be looking for me." As I watched her run down the steps and head up the sidewalk, I realized I'd been right a few minutes before when

I decided she couldn't be trusted. I felt sure had she been asked she would have gladly turned state's evidence.

There I stood alone, on the library steps in my yellow Sunday dress, holding a large loaf of bread in my arms.

The interrogation began as soon as I got in the car. "I don't know where the bread came from." That was my story and I stuck to it. When someone finally asked what I intended to do with a whole loaf of bread, I didn't know that either. Tears didn't help. I was threatened with direr consequences if I didn't tell them how I happen to have a whole loaf of bread in my possession. But they were unable to crack me; it was as if I'd taken the fifth.

I don't remember what happened to the loaf of bread, which was rather a luxury. I eavesdropped on my parents and uncle talking the next night after I was sent to bed. I heard my mother describe how Mr. Court approached her while she was shopping that morning and told her about my shopping spree on Sunday. He just wanted to make sure that it was OK to have let me charge the bread. I think my parents were relieved to find out that I had not actually swiped the bread. I strained to hear what my punishment was going to be as my mother went over the embarrassment I had caused. It was the first, but not the last, of many family discussions centering on what should be done about Mary Lynn. Just as I drifted off to sleep I was pretty sure I heard my uncle and dad laughing.

Look Mom!

1934

In the wonderful world of childhood back in the '30s, a favorite game was called "Let's pretend." It would go like this; Billy to best friend, Alvin, "Let's pretend we're going to Mars. I'll be Buck Rogers and you be Wilma Dearing."

Alvin was not happy. "I want to be Buck Rogers, you be Wilma."

Billy won this time since he suggested the game and they were in his yard. "I said it first and you got to be the Lone Ranger last time, and I was Tonto." So in the back yard, using only their imaginations, Billy and Alvin would become famous heroes and save the world.

"Pretend we are in my space ship and we crash on some unknown planet. You get killed."

"I don't want to get killed; I just get knocked out, OK? Pretend I broke my leg." Alvin hobbled around, using a stick as crutch, ready for action. "Pretend the monster aliens attack us. I'll fight them off with my crutch."

"Pretend I use my sting ray gun and I'll kill all the aliens and save you," yells Billy trying to recapture control. "Zap! Zap! You say 'Oh thank you Buck you are so brave!'" Let's pretend this, pretend that, and you could be anyone or anywhere you wanted to be, just by pretending.

My husband, George, tells this "Pretend" story from his childhood. He and his friend had found a dry ditch and decided to play War. George said, "Let's pretend the Germans are shooting at us. Here comes a bomb!"

Darryl shouted, "Pretend I'm a football player and I jump up and catch the bomb." While *Pretending* you are only limited by your imagination.

The year I was seven, Sally and I would play together after school at either of our homes. I liked playing at her house best as she had a big back yard with a few out buildings and a tree or two. Sally had proved a little untrustworthy the year before during my big shopping spree; however I was willing to give her another chance since her mom always had cookies ready for us after school.

As I recall, Sally and I loved to *Pretend*. She had a supply of baby blankets that made great capes. We could be Flash Gordon and Dale Arden one day and royalty the next. Sally preferred being the queen, which was OK with me, as I knew I was really a long lost princess that my folks had found when I was a baby.

My very favorite was Tarzan, King of The Jungle. Sally let me be Tarzan most of the time so she could be Jane, his beautiful mate. We would climb the low branches of the trees and pretend to swing from limb to limb escaping from the poison darts of the pygmies. Duke, Sally's dog, took on the role of a hungry lion waiting to chase us. Sometimes we would let my little brother play and we made him be Cheetah, our pet chimpanzee.

Sally could climb better than I could, but that didn't stop me from demanding my turn at being Tarzan. At home I practiced climbing in an almond tree at the back of the house. I dearly wanted to be able to out-climb Sally. I talked my older brother into hanging a rope to the higher tree limb. Tarzan used vines, but a rope would be good enough. Grasping the rope I'd push off and swing out reaching for a nearby branch. Grabbing the branch, I let go of the rope and pulled myself up to sit on the limb. I was getting pretty good, so I thought about jumping from one branch to the other without the rope. I'd seen Tarzan do just that in the Sunday funnies. Sometimes he would be carrying Jane or Cheetah would be hanging on to his neck.

I was just trying to work up my nerve when my mother stepped out onto the back porch. I thought, *won't mom be proud of me when she sees how good I am at swinging from the tree.* "Mom, Mom," I shouted, "Watch! me Tarzan!" I pushed off from the fork of the tree, arms out-stretched, reaching for a branch a couple feet away. As my body left the safety of the trunk of the tree I felt like I was flying for a few seconds. I missed the branch by several inches and sprawled full length on the hard ground. All the wind was knocked out of me. I wanted to howl, but I couldn't catch my breath. Blood was coming from my nose.

My mother checked me over and after assuring herself that I had no broken bones, her concern turned to dismay. "Get in the house young lady so I can clean you up. Do you realize, Mary Lynn, you just scared me half to death? You could have killed yourself."

I always knew I was in trouble when I went from Mary to Mary Lynn. Taking my arm and pulling me along, she kept on talking, "I want you to come inside and think about what you just did."

My mother was a great one on thinking. Throughout my childhood I spent a lot of time sitting in a chair in the kitchen thinking about what I had just done! I was still in the chair when my father got home from work. He took one look at me, one look at my mother and said, "I see you are thinking about something you did this afternoon that upset your mother. What was it this time?"

I had a perfect answer ready for him, I had been thinking about it for some time. "I was pretending that I was Tarzan, but I need more practice."

There's Gold in Them Thar Hills

1935

I ran all the way to Sally's house to break the exciting news! "I can't play with you today; we are going to the mountains to find some gold," I announced importantly. However Sally didn't seem impressed.

"That's OK, I'm going to Anna Mae's birthday party, so I couldn't play with you anyway," Sally stated. I never could get the better of Sally. Ever since she got the spoiled milk I'd put in the crate when we were in kindergarten, she had it in for me. I had thought about getting a new best friend, but Sally's mom always had cookies for us when we played in her back yard after school. I would put up with a lot for homemade oatmeal cookies with raisins.

"Where have you been, Mary?" my mother frowned as she rinsed strawberries fresh from our garden. "Have you got your things together? We'll be leaving as soon as your father gets the rabbits dressed and cut up." I hated to think about the cute little bunnies, but I did love fried rabbit. When my mother woke me early this morning and reminded me that we would be going to the mountains to visit relatives at their goldmine I was very excited. I hadn't known we knew such glamorous people.

My brother Floyd had his slingshot tucked in his back pocket. "It's good for squirrel hunting," he explained, "and I got my pocket knife in case we see a bear." He carried out some blankets and tossed them on the back seat of our 1925 Model T Ford. After kicking the front tire, he came back into the kitchen where my mother had the food ready to be loaded. Floyd took the dish of fresh strawberries and a bottle of milk, while I carried the pan of cut up rabbit to the car. Papa had built a cooling box that rested on the running board and was attached to side of the car. It was used for storing dishes and utensils and carrying food when we traveled. The door was hinged on the bottom, and dropped down to form a small table handy for making sandwiches and serving the food. Mom rearranged the items and added a bag of flour, bacon and the fresh eggs she had gathered from our chickens early that morning.

It looked like we were ready to leave when at last Papa appeared with a large watermelon that he carefully set on the floor of the back seat. "You kids keep your feet off that watermelon; I want it to get to Art's in one piece."

Floyd jumped in the back directly behind the driver. "Dibs on the other window!" shouted four-year-old Billy running to the car.

"Mom," I howled, "I never get the window."

"Stop your fighting. You can have the window seat coming home, Mary Lynn." I decided then and there that I would only have two children so they both could have a window while riding in the car. Actually, I decided to have two girls, boys were always so mean-spirited. Papa started the car. Mama sat beside him, half turned so she could keep an eye on the back seat. Floyd was wearing his stupid aviator's helmet and sat poised as the co-pilot. Billy, still with a smirk on his face for having bested me to the window, waved at the neighbor's dog while I sat hunkered down, squashed between the two of them, my skinny legs barely straddling the watermelon. The Chases were off on a big adventure.

While traveling cross-country past Merced, we saw the dark gentle slopes in the distance. I had never noticed the mountains to the east before. From the back seat of the open Model T, they seemed a long way off, and I wondered how many days it would take for us to get to where the gold was. "Are you sure you know where you are going, Lynn?" Mama asked.

My father, who was never the worrier, smiled at her. "I have Art's letter right here with the map he drew. It is about 18 miles north of Coulterville near Blanchard. We won't have any problems." Papa, the eternal optimist, turned his attention to the twisting road.

"Who's Art?" Billy demanded. He had been asleep last night when Mama told us about going to the mountains to visit her uncle. It seems that Art and her brother Forrest, owned a real goldmine up near Yosemite.

"Well, maybe they don't really own it," she continued, "They're actually grubstaked." At my puzzled look she went on to explain. "Grubstaked means you get someone to give you enough money to live on while you work a gold claim." It all sounded mysterious to me.

Floyd chimed in to show how much smarter he was. "Then when Uncle Art finds the gold everyone will be rich."

By now the Model T was working hard, and the radiator boiled over as the road rose steeply towards the summit. At one point the car stalled dangerously close to the edge and my stomach turned over as I looked down hundreds of feet into the rocky ravine.

Pop quietly ordered all of us out of the left side of the car with Mama climbing over the back seat. Once we were safely in the middle of the road he told us to walk to the top of the grade. After putting large rocks under the front tires, to prevent the car from rolling over the edge, he careful turned the car around and began backing up the narrow road. It looked as if the car might slip off the side and go over, so I hid my eyes. However, the Model T seemed to have more power in reverse than in low gear and made it to the top safely. We ran laughing to where Pop waited for us and climbed in once again. A little later we stopped to let the radiator cool down and had a light lunch of some leftover cornbread and water from a nearby stream.

"The food in the cooling box is for when we get to Uncle Art's tonight," mother said when Billy begged for some strawberries. After a walk into the trees, for a potty break, it was time to go. "You kids get in the car; we need to get going if we're to get there before dark."

As the afternoon wore on I could hear my parents having a discussion, Mama began waving the map around. Floyd whispered to me that he thought we were going around in circles. After a bit, things grew quiet in the front seat, Mama sat with her arms folded tightly across her chest with an *I told you so!* look written on her face. Soon papa pulled over and consulted the letter once again. About a mile up the grade he drove the car off the main road and followed two tire tracks down a shallow gorge and with a cry of triumph pulled into a campsite.

After knocking on the makeshift door with no answer, we took off exploring the surrounding area with warnings about not going out of sight of the camp. There wasn't much to see only a few scraggly trees and large boulders scattered about. To one side there was a tired looking vegetable garden, in desperate need of water. The mountain rose directly behind the camp casting long dark shadows. I was disappointed when I couldn't find the goldmine.

It grew late and Uncle Art still hadn't returned, and I was getting hungry. Mama decided she better fix something for us to eat. The door to the shack was unlocked so she, with Billy and me trailing close behind, went in. The room was small (about 9' x 8') with a cooking area close to the door, a rough table with three mix-and-matched wooden chairs, and a cabinet with dishes on one shelf and books on the bottom. The only light came in from the open door. There was a kerosene lantern hanging from a rafter over the table, so when Papa came in he lit it. I looked around and saw an opening at the rear of the room with an old quilt tacked over it, probably leading to the bedroom. Mama fired up the rusty Coleman camp stove as Floyd and I brought in the food. She rolled the rabbit in flour, added bacon grease to the large skillet and dropped in the pieces. Soon the savory smell of frying meat filled the tiny room. Coffee was perking in the pot and bread and sliced tomatoes were on the table when we heard a car drive up.

Through the open door, we saw an old truck pulling next to our Model T. It was hard to tell who was the most surprised when a family with three young children came spilling out of the truck. Papa explained the situation and soon the grown-ups were all laughing about burglars and strangers invading their home, while we children continued to eye one another. "Sure," said Pete, the father, "we know Art and Rose, they have the old Davidson mine on the other side. I'll lead you over so you won't get lost again."

Papa looked sheepishly at Mama and she smiled back at him. "I've got supper about ready, let's all sit down and eat before we go." The young woman went out to a root cellar and brought in apples to add to the table. Pete brought out another lantern from the bedroom, which helped lighten the room. A bench was carried in from outside. By the time supper was over and the dishes done, the two families were no longer strangers.

We set off to find Uncle Art. It had been a long day and by the time we reached his campsite I had fallen asleep and had to be carried into the shack by my Uncle Forrest and put to bed on a pallet of blankets in the corner. I missed all the excitement of recounting the day's happenings. Uncle Forrest was my mother's only brother and fourteen years her junior. To my six-year-old eyes, he was handsome and as dashing as a movie star. Also working the mine was Great Uncle Will, Art's younger brother, who had been born deaf and had never learned to speak. In later years, having known he was referred to as "Dummy" by the townspeople of La Grange, I realized what a sad and lonely life he must have led.

Over bowls of oatmeal the next morning, we learned how Forrest had gotten the *grubstake* from a businessman in Long Beach and with a few dollars had bought the rights to this old mine shaft and all the equipment. When the vein had run out more than 40 years ago, the owners had closed the mine and walked off leaving everything behind. It was now 1933 and we were in the middle of the depression. Jobs were non-existent and even few flecks of gold were worth digging for. Uncle Art explained that many families scattered throughout the hills were hoping to strike it rich. Some, like the family we met last night, had young children who had never seen the inside of a schoolhouse or owned a new pair of shoes.

"These are tough times all over, and while you can dig, there is always hope," he said with a distant look in his eyes. He continued, "A man without hope would be better off dead." I wasn't sure why the room grew so quiet all of a sudden.

Mama and Aunt Rose stayed to clean up the dishes while the rest of us rushed outside to see what a real goldmine looked like. The opening of the mineshaft was located only a few hundred feet from their shack. Forrest took over the role of the guide. "The shaft," he explained, "runs hundreds of feet deep into the mountain." I looked in but could only see about 20 feet ahead. "See the rail tracks? They go clear to the end of the shaft. We're not working that far in. There was a cave-in last year and it is too dangerous."

Papa shook his head. "I don't want any of you kids to go in by yourself. Is that clear?"

Forrest pointed to a big cart with metal wheels sitting on the tracks filled with rocks and ore. "We'll unload the ore this afternoon and show you how we crush the rocks so we can see if there is any gold."

"What's this cable for?' Floyd asked pointing at the end of the cart. The other end of the cable wound around a wrench mounted on an old truck flat bed.

"We push the empty cart down the shaft," answered Forrest pointing at the dark tunnel, "to get to where we are digging. I'll take you down there and you can see how we use pickaxes to chisel rock from the side of the mine. Then we load the heavy pieces into the cart to bring it out."

Uncle Art cranked up a small gas engine that was used to turn the wrench winding the cable. "The cart is very heavy when loaded, so this is how we pull it out here to the entrance," he said looking at the engine with pride. "Some miners still use donkeys, but the engine does it better."

By now Mama had joined us and we got another warning about doing anything foolish. Everyone wanted to be the first to go into the mine, but it was decided that only two at a time should go with my uncle. When it was my time to go I adjusted the miner's cap, with the flashlight attached, to the crown on my head. The heavy battery was carried in a sling draped over my shoulder. Papa and I walked with Forrest down the long cool shaft. The further in we went the darker and colder it became. We each had a headlight, but it was still difficult to see. I heard the sound of water dripping and wondered where the sound was coming from. "Is that water?" I asked.

"It's seeping down the sides of the mine from underground springs." Forrest explained. "Watch where you step, it gets pretty deep in places so it's better if you walk on the high ground between the tracks."

It seemed to me that we walked in a long ways, but at last I saw a flickering light and we finally reached where they had recently been digging. From the first trip in, with Floyd and Billy, my uncle had left a lighted gas lantern hanging from a rock. I looked around and thought about how deep we were under the mountain and remembered what he had said about caves. Forrest swung his heavy pickaxe into the rock wall three or four times and a boulder broke loose and slid to the floor of the cave. I tried to pick it up, but it was too heavy. "Boy," I said, "you guys must want that gold really bad." I decided I probably didn't want to be a gold miner when I grew up.

The damp air and eerie lights scared me. I had seen enough and wished we were back in the sunlight. It was a relief when my uncle said we better go back out.

That afternoon my fanily watched as they moved the rocks and ore from the cart to the rock crusher to be pulverized. When it was pebble size they hauled it in buckets to a sluice in the nearby stream to wash away dirt, always hoping for the glint of gold.

At the goldmine: Blanchard, California

Fall 1934

Back row: Papa, Aunt Rose, and Uncle Jack Sterling
Front Row: Mary, Uncle Forrest, Uncle Art, Billy's head, and Floyd

Mary and Uncle Forrest

Mama and Uncle Forrest

Late in the afternoon a neighbor stopped by; guests were a rarity on the mountain. He brought a big piece of bear meat from a recent kill. "I figured you'd want something special for your kin folks." Aunt Rose sniffed as she thanked him. As she hustled the meat off to the kitchen, I thought I heard her say something about *tough as cow's hide.*

Following an early dinner of beans and potatoes we got ready to go to a local dance. The dance was being held at the Blanchard's one room schoolhouse. The older folks elected to stay at home while Forrest took my parents and us three kids to the dance. Dances with local fiddlers providing the music are big events in the mountains and families came from miles around. The school playground was lit up and children of all ages ran in and out of the schoolroom. Grandmas and sleeping babies shared the benches.

Billy had fallen asleep in the back seat on the way to the dance so I was appointed to check on him from time to time. The play yard was full of running and laughing children of all ages. A well dominated the center of the play yard, with a bucket tied to a rope attached to an overhead pulley. The bucket was dropped down the well and wound up full of cool fresh water.

Mama had a busy time taking turns dancing with Papa and Forrest. I noticed several of the young women trying to catch my uncle's eye, and he never missed a dance. We were exhausted by our busy day and headed back to camp around midnight. As we pulled in next to the campsite, Billy sat up and looked around. "Oh boy!" he exclaimed, "We're there!" We teased Bill for years about missing his first dance.

The next morning a huge tarantula was discovered sunning on some rocks near the outhouse. A tarantula with long hairy legs is truly a scary looking giant spider. Uncle Will tried to demonstrate how they would jump when prodded with a stick, but I guess this one was too sleepy and just sat there.

Floyd and Forrest headed up the stream to do some trout fishing. I'd had enough of the goldmine the day before and persuaded my uncle to let me ride one of his mules he had out to pasture. I finally managed to get on by standing on the split rail fence and draping my leg over his side as my dad led him. I took the rein and made giddyap sounds with mixed results. Not used to having anyone on his back, the mule ignored the pulling of the rein and headed for the nearest tree with low hanging branches. My ride lasted less than a minute when he deliberately walked under the tree and scraped me off.

At lunch, there was talk of rattlesnakes and Aunt Rose demonstrated how she walked through the rocks with a forked stick in case she ran into one. That night we had fresh trout and over-cooked bear roast. It had a very strong wild taste and lived up to Aunt Rose's description of tough as cowhide. The next morning I was covered with an mess of hives and my shoulder was sore from my fall from the mule; I was ready to go home. The only gold that I had seen was some flakes in a small vial that Uncle Will kept in his pocket. We packed up around ten and headed down the mountain. I looked back as we pulled away from their little campsite. My gold mining relatives all stood waving and Aunt Rose was crying. At last I heard her call out, "Hurry back real soon now, you all hear?"

After a bath and a good night's sleep in my own bed I headed over to tell Sally all about my exciting trip to the mountains. I was still covered with hives and my nose was sunburned. Sally came out on her porch with a new set of jacks. It all came out in one sentence. "I looked for gold, saw a tarantula, rode a mule, slept on the floor, and ate bear meat and horse liver."

Without looking at me Sally sat down on the porch and spread out her pretty new jacks. "I got these at Anna Mae's birthday party, just before we had strawberry ice cream and chocolate cake. Wanna play?"

Whidbey Island

1935-1946

Prize Costume

1936

It was the third week in October and excitement filled the crisp fall air. Apples and pears had been picked, wrapped in pages from last years Sears and Roebucks catalog and stored in boxes in the root cellar. Our barn was full of freshly mown hay. Summer was over and night temperatures dipped to the low 30s. Ice formed on the shallow puddles left from the seasonal rain, and I liked the sound of it cracking as I deliberately broke the ice by stepping on it on the way to school. This morning, against my desperate pleas, my mother insisted that I wear my ugly long cotton stockings. Once we left home I rushed ahead of my brothers, not wanting to walk with them. I had a plan.

When I reached the old Maris farm I ducked into an abandoned tool shed and quickly took off the offending stockings and garter belt and stashed them in an empty coffee can. I planned to put them back on after school. Sneaking out of the shed, I fell in step with my little brother Billy. "What were you doing in that old shed? You know we aren't supposed to snoop around these old buildings Mama said. I'm going to tell." Nothing much got past him.

"I was just looking around waiting for you slow-pokes. I wasn't hurting anything." I retorted shivering in the cold air. "Come on, I'll race you down the hill."

It felt good getting inside the warm schoolroom. The room was decorated with orange colored cutouts of jack-o-lanterns, black cats and floating white ghosts that we had made the day before. Halloween was only a little over a week away, after which the decorations would be taken down and we would make paper turkeys, Pilgrims' hats and Indians. As my classmates filed in I waited, but no one seemed to notice that my legs were bare.

After school Marion Webster handed me a small envelope. She was planning a big party and it seemed as if all the kids in the little town of Langley were being invited. *"Prizes for the scariest and for the most original costumes,"* the invitation read. The homemade invitation, made from orange construction paper, was in the shape of a Jack-0-Lantern. I rushed home to show it to my mom, completely forgetting my stockings back at the Maris farm.

This was to be my first ever Halloween party and I couldn't have been more excited. My brother Floyd showed me his invitation shaped like a black cat and we compared notes.

"What are you going to be?" I asked him across the supper table.

"Probably be a pirate," he answered after thinking it over, "all I need is a sword and an eye patch."

"I'm going to be a ghost." Billy announced.

"No imagination!" I sniffed.

"Are you catching a cold, Mary Lynn?" Mom looked at me closely.

I decided it was best to ignore her question. "I'm not sure what costume I'll make for the party. I want to win one of the prizes." I dreamed of goblins and witches on broomsticks until Mom woke me the next morning. She was hurrying me to get dressed by laying out my school clothes. "Where's your garter belt, Mary Lynn?"

"What garter belt?"

"Your garter belt. The one you wore to school yesterday that held your stockings up." She frowned as she went through my dresser draw. "Come to think of it, I don't remember you taking them off when you changed clothes yesterday after school."

I was trying to figure out what was my greatest crime. Was it that I took off my stockings and didn't wear them after she insisted that I should; or was it that I had lost my garter belt? I wasn't sure what I should confess. I decided to stick to my story that the belt had somehow disappeared from my clothes closet. I figured it could magically reappear at some later date and all would be well.

"I guess you will just have to wear your knee socks today until I can find your garter belt. I just hope you don't catch your death of a cold." My mom was a California girl and never got used to the cold and wet weather on Whidbey Island.

Some of my classmates were abuzz with the excitement of the upcoming party. I listened as they talked about what costumes they planned on wearing. I was trying to come up with something no one else thought about. On my way home from school I remembered my stash and thought about how I could get my stockings and garter belt back home without Mom seeing me. One thing I knew for sure was that she would not just forget about them. It was the middle of the depression and I only had one garter belt and two pair of long stockings. I knew the sooner they *magically reappeared* the better. So when I reached the Maris farm I slipped into the old tool shed and found the stockings and garter belt where I had hidden them the day before. As I neared our house I wadded them up and tucked them under my coat. I tried to smooth the large lump that suddenly appeared just below my armpit.

Mom was usually in the living room, listening to *My Gal* Sal on the radio when we came home from school. I decided to try for the back door and attempt to go directly to my room where I could throw the evidence under the bed to *find* it later. I carefully opened the back door and stepped in the kitchen. I made it half way across the room. "Mary Lynn is that you? Why are you coming through the kitchen? Come in here where I can see you."

I thought about making a dash for it, but figured she probably wouldn't notice the large bulge under my coat. This is the kind of stupid decision that has plagued me most of my life. "What do you want? I need to go in and change my clothes."

"Come in the living room, right now."

I slowly walked to the doorway, standing as straight as possible and avoiding her steady look. "Mary, what do you have there?"

"Where? I don't have anything."

"Under your coat. What is that?"

"It's nothing…oh! It's just some homework."

"Bring it over here; why do you have it under your coat?"

Tears don't usually work with Mom, but I turned them on anyway, for the lack of a better plan. After dinner my mom and I sat down for a mother and daughter chat. My question about what was the worse crime was clearly answered. What I had done was not good, but my lying about

25

it only made it much worse. I pleaded a headache and told her that I might be coming down with a cold. There's nothing like admitting that you were wrong to smooth things over.

As punishment I was put on restriction and there was a threat of my not being able to attend the Halloween party, but I got time off for good behavior. I'd had plenty of time to think about my costume and about decided to go as a gypsy.

In the Sunday funnies I spotted *Tillie The Toiler* going to a costume party. The comic strip is about a young businesswoman living and working in the city. In today's paper she was outfitted in a dress made from old newspapers and looked glamorous. I could just picture myself swishing into Marion's party and everybody admiring my ingenuity.

The evening of the party finally arrived. Floyd had made himself a wooden sword and fashioned an eye patch. He dug out an old hat of Mama's and stuck a turkey feather in the brim. Billy cut eyeholes in his white flour sack and stumbled around until Pop suggested he cut holes for his arms so he would have balance.

I had a stack of newspapers and the pincushion. I stood impatiently in front of Mama while she draped the sheets of paper around me and pinned them together. When I raised my arms or tried to walk, the paper tore and she had to redo them. Finally she stepped back and studied the effect. "I guess if you take little steps and keep your arms at your sides you will be OK."

I rustled as I minced my way over to look in the mirror. I expected to see something like the curvaceous silhouette of *Tillie The Toiler,* but I was disappointed. I looked pretty ridiculous and I had stuck myself several times with the pins. I wanted to cry. This was not at all as I had imagined I would look, but it was too late to change now.

"Come on, we have got to go or we'll be the last ones there," Floyd yelled as he edged toward the door.

"You look pretty dumb," Billy commented from under his flour sack.

I viewed my options, but no way would I miss my first Halloween party. So the three of us started out down the path with Floyd in the lead, singing "Ho! Ho! Ho! A bottle of rum," running his sword through the lilac bushes and ordering it to "walk the plank." Billy was close on his heels practicing his "Boo," and then me, trying not to prick myself and taking little mincing steps.

About half way to Marian's house it began to sprinkle and by the time Floyd knocked on her door it was a downpour. We were soaked and the black ink from the newspaper began to run. I had gotten a lot of smudges on my hands trying to hold my costume together. I moved to a corner of the living room as my costume came apart.

Several girls gathered around the cute pirate and Mrs. Webster suggested that Billy take off his ghost costume so he could bob for apples. I stayed in the corner wiping my face and hair. When the time came to judge the costumes, I had gotten rid of most of the newspaper and my face and hair were streaked with the black ink. I had accepted the fact that my costume was not going to win any prize.

Mr. Idle, the school principal, and Mr. and Mrs. Webster were the judges and they had everyone line up as they walked back and forth looking very serious until finally they were ready. Bob Rinehart in his Frankenstein getup received the prize for the "Scariest." Sammy De Bryan was voted the "Ugliest," as a haggled-toothed witch. No one was surprised when Evelyn Cook was voted the most original as an Indian maiden.

"Attention everyone, we decided to give another prize." Everyone looked expectantly at Mr. Idle. "This is for the *worst ever costume* and that prize goes to little Mary Chase."

Nature's Rhythm

The snow had melted, but it was still too early for any signs of spring. February was an exciting month for my 5th grade class. First, there was Valentine's Day with a party at school on the 14th, followed closely by a vacation day on Abraham Lincoln's Birthday, and then George Washington's Birthday on the 22nd. Cutout silhouettes of the presidents' profiles lined the wall over the blackboard.

My fifth grade teacher, Mrs. Johnson, had asked several students to decorate a large cardboard box for the party on Valentine's Day. Red and white crepe paper covered the square box, with cutouts of hearts and cupids pasted on the sides. A few days before the party, the box was placed in front of the room, where we dropped in the valentines for exchanging with our special friends. The day of the party the box was opened and the valentines were passed out. It wasn't unusual for a few popular kids to get many more valentines than others. The ultimate thrill was to receive one from the cutest boy in class. As I counted the valentines sent to me, I checked to see who had sent them. I noticed that Leona Mellings, the prettiest girl in class, had twice as many valentines as I did. But, I had gotten a little heart shaped card from Eugene. We had homemade frosted cookies and fruit punch for refreshments.

At home, my brother Floyd, and I were involved in 4-H. Last year he had bought a piglet and was raising her to show at the county fair in September. He had built a pigpen out past the garden area, with a small shelter. He fed the young sow garbage, from the school lunchroom, and added a bucket of grain and excess milk. My 4-H project was all about a vegetable garden, meal planning, cooking and canning, which I was expected to do anyway.

On those cold winter days, we stayed close to the wood burning stove in the living room. After an early supper our entire family, spent most evenings listening to the radio, reading, playing cards or Monopoly, and doing school work. A special event was when President Roosevelt delivered his famous *Fireside Chat*. We all gather close to the little Philco table radio and Pop would demand total silence while his hero addressed the nation. The late thirties was a changing time. Roosevelt had brought us out of the devastating depression with programs, such as the Work Program Administration (WPA) and the Civilian Conservation Corp (CCC), only to be faced with the war clouds gathering over Europe.

March brought heavy storms with torrents of rain and wind, keeping everyone indoors for much of the time. The relentless rain soaked the ground and loosened the roots of the large fir trees. Often, during a storm, the wind would uproot trees, taking down the power lines. Many times during these storms we would be without electricity and in darkness for several days. And then a break; the sun would come out for a few days giving us a false hope of spring. Out came the seed catalogues, along with thoughts of plowing, planting and a bountiful harvest.

By April, Pop would plow and disc our garden area, adding animal manure as natural fertilizer. Then, he and Floyd would level and worked the soil until it was time to plant. We watched the mail for the packets of seeds. Early planting consisted of fast growing lettuce, carrots, beets, tomatoes, onions and radishes. Pole beans, squash, and potatoes took longer to mature and needed several feet of garden space. Mama and I cut the potatoes, which had been stored in our root cellar all winter, into quarters. A potato plant would grow from each small piece. With the planting done, we waited for the sun and Mother Nature to work the miracle of small seeds sprouting and pushing through the soil and growing into plants.

Mama was a baseball fan and her team was the Seattle Rainer's. She had a friendly feud with her father, who rooted for the Los Angeles Angels. She sat near the radio, listening to Leo Lassen, the announcer from Seattle, cheering her team on. Leo made the game so real that you felt you were at the ballpark. I went to bed many nights with his excited voice in the background. When a batter hit a homerun it was "It's going, going, it's gone!" with the roar of the crowd in the background. If the Rainers beat the Angels my mother would write a note to her father teasing him about the victory.

May was cold and wet that year. The first grade class performed a May Pole Dance around the flagpole. Dressed in colorful costumes, dancing and weaving in and out, the children wound the crepe paper streamers of different colors around the pole. I believe that was the last year our school held the dance. For some reason the May Pole and May Day baskets celebrations faded away.

As the last day of school approached, I had mixed feelings. The school was consolidated and classmates were bused from isolated communities, so I would not see many of my classmates until the next school year began in September. On the last day of school, we had refreshments, our report cards were handed out, and we were let out early; it was the third of June and Floyd's fourteenth birthday.

Tender shoots were pushing through the wet soil by now and my brothers and I were responsible for chopping down the weeds between the rows of growing plants. This seemed to be a never-ending job, for no matter how hard we chopped, by the next week, it all had to be done again. With June came strawberry season. This year Floyd and I picked berries for the Lipton family to earn money for school clothes. Mom had a seasonal job at the strawberry plant located near the Langley dock. Growers brought the flats of berries to the cannery, weighed and dumped them in a large holding tank. Once washed the berries were moved on a conveyer belt past women standing on either side, who culled and threw out the undesirable debris. The belt moved the berries through another quick wash, and then they were finally packed in large wooden barrels and covered with sugar. The barrels were shipped by truck to a plant on the mainland, where the strawberries were made into jam and other delicacies.

By the middle of June we were enjoying leaf lettuce, radishes, green onions and baby carrots from our own garden. It was time to teepee the poles over the bean plants so the vines could climb. We had a big Royal Anne Cherry tree at the side of the house. Billy picked a couple buckets of the delicious cream and pink fruit making enough for Mama and me to can up 10 or 12 jars. After the first pick, we were allowed to invite friends over to climb to the top branches to eat our fill of the cherries.

Times seemed simpler in 1938, and once our chores were done, we were pretty much free to roam the countryside. I loved the woods behind our property and spent many long hours there. The sound of the wind moving through the trees was my only companion. I claimed as my hideout, an old one-room log cabin, with a small brook close by. The cabin had a dirt floor and no covering for the windows, but it was my secret place. I sat on a nearby tree stump listening to the water and daydreamed. I'm sure others knew the cabin was there, but I never shared it with anyone else.

More than anything else I loved to swim and much of my free time, during the summer, was spent with friends at the beach or at Goss Lake. The frigid waters of Puget Sound didn't faze me. We often had spontaneous beach parties. Campfires, fashioned from driftwood, brightened the summer sky and swimmers would huddle around, soaking up the warmth. The word spread somehow and kids from all over would show up, and presto, it was party time. Whoever thought of getting together would be responsible for the buns and mustard. Someone would bring marshmallows and each person was responsible for bringing their own wieners. Lights, from fishing boats anchored off shore, bobbed as the boat rocked with the waves. Sometimes ghost stories were exchanged, but I liked it best when we would sing the songs learned at camp. Teens were beginning to pair off, to disappear into the night, and do whatever teenagers have always done; leaving the younger ones wishing we were sixteen. Our favorite beach was across town from our house, below the De Bryun's property. Our youth church group, with the help of our pastor, had built a bathhouse at the bottom of the cliff. It was here that I first tried to smoke little pieces of driftwood.

Goss Lake, said to be bottomless, was out about seven miles from Langley. It was a special treat when we got together as a group for a day at the lake. Located off the Saratoga Road, it was remote with no houses within a couple miles. Someone had built a raft, with a diving board, that was anchored about thirty feet from shore. I can't say for sure, but it was rumored that a small group of young people had once skinny-dipped, on the far side of the lake.

Mary, 10, Sandy Point WA 1937

Billy, my younger brother was the family fisherman. Whenever weather permitted, you could find him on the Langley dock with his pole, tackle box, bait, and a great deal of patience. He brought home saltwater perch, occasional cod and crabs from his crab net. The rules of our house were that if you caught it, you cleaned it, and then Mama would cook it for our dinner. I often joined him, but never had the patience to spend an entire afternoon staring at the blue-gray water under the dock waiting for a bite.

Bill, 11; Catch at Langley dock 1940

In the pasture and woods behind our house, wild blackberries grew with abundance. In July and August, Mama would make cobblers for desert and jam and jelly for the winter. Plums were plentiful, and one of my favorite spreads was plum butter. I was expected to help mom with the canning which fed us through the winter. We put up string beans, corn, pears and applesauce in quart mason jars. Cabbage was made into sauerkraut and kept in a large stone crock. Later, baskets of potatoes, onions, carrots and Hubbard Squash would go in our root cellar along with boxes of late Pippin Apples. Even at this young age I would get a sudden feeling of comfort, as I looked at the rows of freshly canned vegetables and fruit, filling the shelves in the cellar.

A smoke house was built near the woodshed, and in the fall Pop, with Floyd's help, butchered a hog. Mama fried the liver, with onions, for dinner, and boiled the heart and tongue. The heart was for sandwiches and the tongue was pickled. Using a bone saw and large knives Pop cut the meat into family size portions. We had pork steak, cutlets, roasts, and baby back ribs, which were double wrapped for the meat locker. A tub of fat was brought into the house, to be rendered for lard the next day. The butt and shoulder roasts went into the smokehouse where a low fire of alder and apple tree wood was kept going 24 hours a day for several weeks until the pork was cured. The large hams and several slabs of bacon were wrapped in clean gunnysacks and hung in the cellar. The hogs head was given to a neighbor; Mama put her foot down and refused to make head cheese, considered a delicacy by many. The smokehouse would be used again to make venison jerky and smoked salmon.

School was scheduled to start the Tuesday after Labor Day and I poured over the Montgomery Ward's and Sears and Roebuck catalogs. I would need lots of new clothes, since I had grown so much taller. Between the money I had saved from picking berries, and what my folks were able to spare, I had enough to start. I mailed in my order to Montgomery Ward's. I waited impatiently for my tea rose underwear, a pair of brown oxfords, two pretty new dresses, and several pairs of knee high socks to arrive. Last year's coat would have to do, for the time being.

I entered the sixth grade and was glad to see all my classmates. Mrs. Johnson was my teacher for the second year. Floyd started high school and Bill was in the fourth grade. He let us know that he was no longer Billy, and he wanted to be called Bill.

The middle of September was the exciting Island County Fair. The year before, WPA workers had built a huge log exhibit hall on county property above the school grounds. The beautiful building still stands and is used today, 70 years later. The Farmers' Country Fair was typical for the time and run by a board of directors. A large outbuilding was filled with livestock where men gathered to smoke their hand-rolled cigarettes and to swap stories. There was a certain friendly competition for the coveted blue ribbon. Prominent cattle ranchers were the judges of the livestock. The youths of FFA and 4-H brought their animals and waited for the auction on the last day. I saw my older brother grooming his fat sow and secretly hoped he would win.

Inside the log exhibition hall, tables covered every inch of floor space. They were loaded with rows of canned fruit and vegetables, dozen of baskets of fresh apples and pears sat along the far wall. An entire section contained different kinds of squash and bright orange pumpkins. On separate tables were beautiful flower arrangements with vivid splashes of color. Two, 30-foot tables held mouth-watering baked goods, the pride of the farmer wives. I found the upside-down cake that I had entered as part of my 4-H project. It sat alone, looking insignificant, and I noticed that it listed to one side. Handmade quilts, needlework and crafts were displayed on the wall. This was the first year that local artists had a separate section. Oils, charcoal and watercolor paintings added a festive look. I saw several seascapes painted by Carolyn Cook who was two grades ahead of me in school.

Near the front entrance I stood fascinated, seeing two totem poles at least ten feet tall. They were hand-crafted and each was hacked out from a single log. Wild animal and Indian symbols had been carefully carved into the wood and painted with bright colors. The tallest was topped with a bald eagle in full flight. The local artist, Mr. Cunningham had made many of these traditional Indian totem poles over the years, but these were probably his finest work. He later donated them to the fair association and they stand today, guarding the entrance gate.

There were several teams of judges. I noticed the town mayor, several teachers and members of the Grange sporting ribbons, announcing their important job. The judging took place during the afternoon of the first day, and by the next morning all the winning ribbons were on display. Ribbons proclaiming Grand Prize, First Place, Second Place, Third Place and Honorable Mention were prominently displayed for all to see. My offering won Second Place and a bright red ribbon. I was pleased until I realized that my upside down cake was the only one in that category.

A small carnival sprang up overnight and boasted a mid-sized ferris wheel and merry-go-round that filled the air with loud music. I had been warned to watch out for gypsies; who often traveled with carnivals. Aunt Katie took me aside, touching my straight white hair and explained that gypsies particularly liked little girls with blond hair. Booths with cupid dolls and stuffed animals lined the mid-way and tempted the unwary. "Come try your luck!" the barker shouted. "One thin dime and you can win this lovely teddy bear for your sweetheart." I liked the booth with brightly colored balloons tied to a backdrop. All you had to do was throw a dart, and pop the balloon; the more balloons you hit the bigger the prize. It looked so easy! "Here you are, little lady, five darts for ten cents."

One side of the hall was the kitchen, where wonderful smells wafted throughout the building. For over thirty years the Grange used the fair as their major fundraiser event. They offered hotdogs and hamburgers with all the trimmings, homemade potato salad, pies, coffee and sodas. Aunt Katie and Uncle Lon spent most of their time working in the booth and watching the crowd push among the exhibits. On the second day, out of money, I hung around hoping to get a free hotdog.

On Sunday, the last day of the fair, Floyd's year-old sow won the blue ribbon for the 4-H group. At auction, he got top dollar for Suzie. Now he would be able to pay off his feed bill and have a little left for himself. Trucks wheeled in around five o'clock. Bill and I watched while the roustabouts took down the ferris wheel and merry-go-round and loaded the parts on the flat beds. What had appeared so glamorous, two days ago, took on a seedy look. I felt a sudden emptiness or sadness, but felt better as we headed home. By Monday morning all signs of the carnival and exhibits were gone, I was in Mrs. Johnson's classroom and life was back to normal.

Indian summer is my favorite time of the year and is spectacular in the northwest. The air was turning crisp; warm sweaters were needed in the early morning and late afternoon. Apples and pears were ripe. We had stored three boxes of them in the root cellar for later use. Mom made the best apple pie in town and she found many other ways to use the abundant crop. One day, Pop, Bill and I gathered several bushels of Pippin apples from our orchard and took them over to Uncle Lon's barnyard. There he had an old wooden apple press. I had never before realized what it was used for. After running water over the apples, they were dumped whole, core and all, in the funnel on top. Pop turned the wheel and the apples were ground and pressed. The amber fluid dribbled out into a large glass container. It took many apples to make a quart of juice. The pulp dropped down into a bucket and was later fed to the pigs. Bill and I both drank our fill of the fresh juice. That night I had the backhouse trots. The juice was sealed in fruit jars and set aside to turn into cider.

On October 3, my father turned 40 years old. Then on October 10, my parents' 17th wedding anniversary, I turned 11. Our family had been living on Whidbey Island for four years and thought of it as our home. Mama still missed California; her parents and sisters' families all lived there. She had not seen any of them since we left Livingston, California, in August of 1935. I realize now, how homesick she probably was. She was raised a California girl and let us know that she hated the constant rain and cold wind.

It was time for Pop, Floyd and Bill to get in our winter supply of wood. Pop had mounted a buzz saw blade on the back of the flat bed of a truck. They had hauled in a large load of fir logs. Pop was feeding the logs into the blade, cutting them to stove length. Floyd was catching the log and tossing them in a pile. It was a cold and windy day with a promise of rain before nightfall. They were wearing gloves and Floyd had on his old jacket. I was in the house, but could see them working from the kitchen window. Floyd caught the log, reached over the saw and gave it a toss. The spinning teeth of the buzz saw caught the sleeve of his jacket and pulled his arm into the blade. Shedding the cloth, the blade cut deep across the back of his wrist. I could hear him yell and saw Pop grab his arm.

I stepped outside to see what was happening and heard my mother cry out behind me. She grabbed a dishtowel and ran over to where Floyd was slumped holding his arm. She wrapped the towel around his bleeding wrist. The towel quickly turned bright red and blood dripped on the ground. I was sent in the house to get a bath towel and handed it to my mother. She covered his arm without removing the blood soaked dishtowel. I could not bring myself to look at Floyd's white face, as I was sure that he had cut off his hand. Mama and Pop had a quick discussion about what to do and where to take him. They didn't trust the only doctor within 50 miles, who was semi-retired anyway, but were afraid Floyd night bleed to death if he didn't get immediate attention. Pop ushered Floyd into the front seat of our old car and drove off towards town.

When Pop got Floyd to the doctor's office he was told he would have to wait, the doctor was busy with another patient. The way I heard the story was that Pop pushed past the doctor's wife and barged in, finding the old man visiting with a lady and drinking tea. My father, not a large man, nor one who ever went looking for trouble, reached down and pulled the old man to his feet and said, "Take care of my son now, or you won't live to regret it." The cut was very deep and across the entire back of his wrist. Luckily neither the bone nor any major tendon was involved. The doctor stitched the jagged wound and bandaged his wrist. It left a terrible scar, but he eventually regained full use of his hand.

November 3rd was Bill's 9th birthday. Thanksgiving was spent at Aunt Katie and Uncle Lon's house that year. Our extended family took turns having dinner for the holidays. I was pleased it was at their house. My aunt, besides being the town gossip, was probably the best cook. The dinner table was loaded with ham, turkey, roast beef, several kinds of potatoes, a variety of vegetables, delicious gravy, home-made rolls and cranberry sauces. For dessert she had made three kinds of pies, fruitcake and cookies. Besides family, she included several old timers who otherwise would have been alone.

We rose from the table, stuffed from the wonderful meal. I helped gather the dishes and carried them into the kitchen. The men wandered into the living room, unfastened the top of their pants and brought out their cigars and cigarettes. As they settled back, the stories began. I had heard most of them time and time again over the last four years. My Uncle Harold had a fascination for bulls and insisted on detailing gory incidents. If you have ever listened to a group of men spinning tales you know they play "one up pence," with each story a little wilder than the one before. These stories of bulls goring farmers made a terrible impressions on me, and I have been deathly afraid of bulls ever since.

My folks were avid readers, for as long as I can remember; Floyd and I followed their example at an early age. I visited the town library every Saturday for a new supply of books. My cousin, Esther, was the librarian and recommended books she thought I might like. The library was small with a tiny budget for new books. I reread my favorites; *A Girl of the Limberlost, Freckles* and the *Emily* and *Jeanne* series, many times. Floyd had a small collection of Big Little Books that he guarded very carefully, but I would sneak them to read when he was off on his bike. The radio was still our biggest entertainment and during Christmas vacation I listened to some of the soap operas. I remember *Ma Perkins, Our Gal*

Sunday, Mary Noble, Back Stage Wife, Just Plain Bill, and *Helen Trent.*
Pretty mild stuff compared to the soap operas of today.

Beginning in early December, I took an interest once again in church.
I'd like to think it was because of the birth of Christ, but to be honest
it was probably in anticipation of the Christmas pageant and the little
bag of candy with an orange, that was usually given out. As Christmas
approached, the tiny town of Langley took on a magical look of earlier
times. A thirty-foot fir tree with hundreds of colored lights dominated
First Street, near The Dog House. Vic Primavera's Star Store, Mortanson
Hardware Store and the Langley Drugstore Store filled their windows
displays with tinsel and bright gift items.

Floyd went into the woods behind our house and brought out a small
tree. It sat on the table in the living room waiting to be decorated. Mom
got out our small box of Christmas decorations that she kept on a shelf
in her closet. It was exciting to un-wrap the colored glass balls. Each
year it was as if I was seeing them for the first time. Bill and I each had
our favorites. First the single strand of lights was wound through the
branches, then the six or seven ornaments and ropes of silver garland.
Finally we covered the branches with tinsel. After supper, when everyone
gathered in the living room, it was time for the show. The overheard light
was turned off and the tree lights were plugged into the extension cord.
We stood spellbound looking at the tree.

"Oh, isn't it beautiful?" "I like the blue ones the best." "No I think
the red are the prettiest." "I'm sure it is our best tree yet." The wonder of
the season filled the room. "Better turn them off and save the lights for
Christmas," Floyd advised.

I bought an oval shaped Pyrex casserole dish for my mother at the
hardware store. Then I counted my small savings, and decided to go to
the secondhand store. I bought a used ashtray for Pop, and painted it a
shiny black. I saw just the thing for Bill who was trying to train his hair
to lay back off his forehead. He had taken to wearing a skullcap, made
from one of Mom's old rayon stockings, to bed. I decided the 10 cents
I had to pay for a large bottle of red Brilliantine hair oil was a gift he
would really use. I wrapped a domino set that looked practically new for
Floyd. I remember how proud I was of the gifts I had picked out, now
under the tree waiting for Christmas Eve.

I was a shepherd in the church pageant Sunday morning before
Christmas. As we expected, after the play, we were each given a small
bag with a nectarine and sticky hard Christmas candy. I had it all

eaten before I had reached home afterwards. On Christmas Eve we traditionally opened our presents. After an early supper we sat around the tree. Bill passed out the gifts. Aunt Katie had come for the event as she most often did. I loved her presents, they were carelessly wrapped and you always figured out what was in the package before it was opened. Cousin Esther gave the family a box of Kleenex. It was the first one we had ever had. Floyd was quite a craftsman and had made something during shop at school for each of us. I watched as my family opened the gifts I had painstakingly chosen. Pop studied the black ashtray and lit a cigarette. Floyd challenged anyone to a game of dominos, and Bill went looking for a mirror. He came back, his hair a little greasy. Everyone was impressed by my gifts. It's funny; I have no recollection of what I received that year, but remember how my mother smiled at me after opening her present and seeing the pretty bowl.

January, 1939, was cold and wet, and Langley had one light snowfall that year. Fred Astaire and Ginger Rogers were playing at the Clyde Theater along with The Three Stooges. I read, in a movie magazine, that Hollywood had made a movie from the book *Gone with the Wind*. There was talk of tearing down the old grade school to make room for a bigger one. Classes would be held in the fair building as the new school was being built. Lefty Smith and Chuck Burke opened a gas station and hamburger stand across the road from the high school. Uncle Lon gave Floyd a bicycle, so I got his old one.

We were all a year older, and wondering what 1939 would bring. Lyle Peterson, a hell, fire and damnation preacher had settled in Langley, splitting the membership of the community church. Buddy, our half Coonhound dog, became ill with distemper and. had to be put to sleep. I joined the local Campfire Girls and planned on becoming a member of Rainbow Girls, when I turned 12 the next October. Floyd was sweet on Silvia DeBryun. Bill, with his best friend Ludlow Lambert would disappear with their dogs into the woods or go to the beach. My folks were looking at some property out near Freeland. It was undeveloped with second and third year growth of timber and acres of brush. The most intriguing feature was the small lake with fresh-water perch.

It was fast approaching February once again; I had a secret crush on Jack, star of our baseball team, and was thinking about making a special Valentine to give to him at the school party. Some things are slow to change. It was wonderful to be almost 12 years old in 1939 and to grow up on Whidbey Island.

**Floyd 14, Mary 11, Bill 9, Uncle Lon's barn in background
Langley 1939**

Keepsies

1938

It seemed like a good way to get even with my brother Floyd at the time.
For what I have no idea. It was my friend Sally's idea. I had Floyd's prize
bag of marbles and we decided to bury all of them in the dirt at the side of
the house. "Mary Lynn did you or did you not bury your brother's marbles
in the yard?" My mother had a way of asking questions when she already
knew the answer. Now, here I was trying to find them by digging around
in the soft dirt.

"No supper until you find every last one of them." Mom always seemed
to favor my brother. She wasn't interested in all the horrible things he had
done to me. Sally heard her mother calling and took off like the little fair
weather friend she was. I don't remember if I found them all or not, but I
did learn not to mess with someone else's bag of "mibs."

By the time I was about nine I had my own bag of "mibs." I had a
large steelie for lagging, several aggies, a small peewee, my prize cats-eye
and assorted colorful glass shooters. Most little girls had a skate key hung
around their neck and a bag of jacks. The boys had the skate key and a
bag of marbles. I had all three. I was one of the few girls in town who
suffered the consequence of having only brothers to play with most of the
time. Sometimes we played just for fun, returning marbles to the original
owner at the end of the game. If you agreed at the beginning of the game

to play for *Keeps,* the winner would keep all that he had shot out of the pot. My brother Floyd was a serious player and I never played against him. If I lost all my marbles to some boy I would tell Floyd and talk him into challenging the winner and get my marbles back.

At school the boys played out behind the gym at recess time. Playing for keeps was forbidden at school, but there were a few diehards. One windy day I joined the boys at lunch break and got into a game of *knuckle down*. We drew a fish-shaped pot and each player would place three to five marbles in the center. From about 12 feet back we lagged at the pot, and the one whose marble came closest to the center of the pot got to shoot first. The object of the game was to knock the marble outside of the pot. If you hit the opponent's shooter you would get another turn. This day my shooter was hot. I cleaned up the first pot in record time and was challenged by Stanley Wilson, the *marble marvel.* By the time the bell sounded and we had to return to the classroom I had double the marbles in my bag and had Stanley, the *marble marvel,* shaking his head.

Some snitch told the teacher that I had taken all of his marbles in a game of keeps. As soon as class started Mrs. Johnson called me in front of the room and demanded that I give the marbles I had won back to the crybaby, ex-marble marvel...my name for him...not Mrs. Johnson's. Not only that, she confiscated my entire bag of *mibs*. "I'm doing this," she explained, "to teach you a lesson."

"It's not fair! He was playing too." My logic failed to convince her of the injustice of punishing me. Mrs. Johnson didn't think girls should play marbles.

"A collie down is not a collie beaten," wrote Albert Peyson Terhune, in my favorite book, *Lad, a Dog,* and with that resolve I was determined to build up my supply of shooters. I needed an easy mark and when I saw Richard *Hard Luck Clyde,* going home from school, I knew I was on my way. I challenged *Hard Luck* to a game of keeps.

The Clyde family was our next-door neighbors with a tall fence separating our two properties. My brother Floyd and Richard had built a ladder over the fence so we had shortcut back and forth. I went over the fence and was back in a few minutes with a bag of marbles I had borrowed from my younger brother. Richard and I started playing in his driveway and it wasn't long before I had doubled my stash. As I was putting them all into my marble bag his father drove up from work, and we moved to the side so he could park.

Norman Clyde was a big man, with a dark five o'clock shadow and a perpetual scowl on his face. I was more than a little afraid of him, although he probably had never said more than a half dozen words to me. Instead of going directly into the house, he came over to where we were standing and asked Richard what was going on. When *Hard Luck* told him he'd just lost all of his marbles to me, Mr. Clyde gave me a sharp look and with a fierce growl turned on Richard. "How could you let a girl beat you?"

I felt sorry for poor *Hard Luck* and stood studying the ground trying to get enough courage to make a run for home. I turned and took a couple steps toward the fence. "Wait a minute Mary, where do you think you are going?"

I wanted to tell him I thought I was going home, but was afraid to say anything. I looked longingly towards the ladder, wondering if I could make my escape.

"So you like to play marbles, do you?" I couldn't believe he was talking to me but swallowed hard and nodded my head. "Come on I'll show you how a real man plays marbles." He sent Richard into the house for some ammunition. By this time *Hard Luck* had a sly smirk on his face and I figured I was in for it. I didn't want to play any more, I just wanted to throw my winnings back at him and run home and put on my pink pinafore.

It didn't take Mr. Clyde very long to clean me out. I am not sure if he was a good player or that I was shaking so badly I couldn't shoot straight. When I got home I had to explain to my mother what had happen. Her mouth grew grim when I told how Mr. Clyde challenged me to play and won all of my brother's marbles and the ones I had won from Richard. I went to my room to think about all the injustices of the world.

When Papa got home from work, around five o'clock, I heard him and Mama arguing in the kitchen. "Don't do it Lynn," she pleaded.

I couldn't hear what Papa said, but it sounded a bit like teaching the big bully a lesson. Oh my gosh! I wondered if he was going to challenge Mr. Clyde to a fight. Mr. Clyde was much bigger of the two and if Papa got hurt it would be my fault. I ran to the bedroom window and tried to see what was going on.

About twenty minutes later I saw Papa coming up our walk and heard him come back into the house. He said something to my mother that I couldn't hear and then came into my room.

He stood in the doorway and gave me a long look. Shaking his head he walked to where I was sitting on my bed. "Get washed up for supper,

Mary." He tossed my brother's bag of marbles on my bed. "You better get these back to your brother."

I looked at the bag. "Thanks Pop," was all I could think to say. I really wanted to ask what had happened next door, but decided to let well enough alone.

As I was trying to return the bag of marbles to my brother's room, he came in. "What are you doing with my marbles?" he demanded. "I'm going to tell mom you were trying to swipe my stuff."

"Oh, shut up! I wasn't trying to steal anything. I was just looking at your *aggies*."

"You better not have taken any, or I really will tell Mom," he threatened as he looked through the bag. "I don't remember having this many before…."

Nothing more was said about marbles at the supper table. After I had finished the dishes I stepped outside and heard a banging that seemed to be coming from the other side of the fence that divided our property and the Clyde's.

Floyd came up to stand beside me, "Well, there goes the friendship ladder."

On Our Way To Riches

1940

"Wait'll you see what Pop just brought home," was my brother Bill's greeting as he ran to meet me. I had stayed after school to practice my tennis serve. The big game was coming up soon between Mabel (Able) Carr and myself, and there wasn't a chance in the world of beating her, unless I could ace her on my serves. Mabel was the eighth grade tennis champ and I was the seventh grade upstart that had somehow made it to the finals.

I could see Bill, all puffed up with some important news, as he cut through the orchard and came running up to me. "What did Pop bring home this time?" I asked, only half interested, my mind still on my practice session at the tennis court.

Two years my junior, Bill and I shared many adventures and family secrets. "You'll never guess in a million years." Grinning, he fell into step with me. When I failed to rise to the bait he continued, "I know you can't, but try to guess anyway. Bet you a penny you can't guess." He finally had my attention.

"You're on; it's a penny if I guess in ten guesses. Right?" I figured I knew what would get my little brother so excited. Our family dog died last year and I had been begging for another one ever since. "Is it a new dog?" I asked hopefully. He shook his head negatively and his smile turned

45

smug. "I know," I said watching his face. "It's a new pig for Floyd to raise for 4-H?'

"No, no it's not a dog and it's not a pig. That's two, try again."

"Give me a hint. Is it something to eat?" I asked, still not too interested.

Bill kept shaking his head and grinning broadly. "You'll never guess. Give up? You might as well pay up now…give me my penny and I'll tell you."

"Well tell me this, is it alive?" With this last guess Bill started howling with laughter. I couldn't understand what was so funny about my question. I wanted to wipe that smug smile off his freckled face and thought about hitting him with my tennis racket. "Give me a hint," I pleaded. He picked up an apple that had fallen from a tree, and threw it at the fence post, shaking his head. "Well, what did Mom say when she saw what Pop brought home?"

Bill looked down at his feet, still grinning. "I don't think she was too happy. She said something about a migraine and went to the bedroom. I haven't seen her since."

Pop was the dreamer and optimist in our family. As long as I knew my father, he never gave up the dream of making the big one. He went from one venture or scheme to the next after hearing about something new to make money. He liked to start a project, but quickly became bored and moved on. He never was one for details, which often caused major problems. Like the time he bought an old commercial fishing boat intent on catching mud sharks that frequented the waters around Sandy Point.

Pop had heard that there was a big market for fish oil. So it seemed an easy way to make some extra money, which we sorely needed. That he had never been aboard a commercial fishing boat, nor had any idea how he would market the fish, if and when he caught any, didn't faze him.

"It's a great opportunity to make a lot of money. A guy at work told me they were paying top price over on the main land. He is getting me the name of the company that wants to buy the sharks." He glanced around the table looking for support. Floyd had his head down; Mom was frowning, while Billy could hardly sit still. Owning a fishing boat, I had visions of cruising around the harbor while all my friends looked on jealously.

Reaching for the bowl of fried potatoes Pop took to a second helping, and automatically put more salt on them. He went on, "I figure it should be a two man operation, handling the boat and the fish net. We can go out whenever I'm off work."

My mom was usually a team player and had in the past, grudgingly helped him in many of his schemes. Pop was the idea man, while Mom usually ended up being the doer. I could see her lips tightening and with a determined look she went on record, "I flatly refuse to go out on a boat I haven't even seen. God knows what condition it will be in." Even Pop could see that she had her mind set as she continued, "I have no wish to drown in the cold waters of Puget Sound; I'm a California girl, after all."

Undaunted, Pop surveyed the remaining three at the table By the process of elimination my older brother Floyd was the designated first mate, and never one to be left out, I announced that I would be the cabin boy. Billy started to protest, but my mother put her foot down for the second time. "You are too young, so just forget about it."

By the next day I was pretty excited, we had never owned a boat before. I could tell Floyd was beginning to like the idea of standing on the deck and waving to the girls on the beach. He wrote down what I should call different parts of the boat for me to memorize. "When I say go *aft* you need to move to the back of the boat, *bow* means the front." The list grew longer, *starboard* is the right side, *port* means left side of the boat. I could tell he planned on taking the First Mate job seriously and was looking forward to ordering the Cabin Boy around. No matter...

With a sense of adventure I went with Pop and Floyd to Double Bluff where we inspected the *Lucky,* which had been in dry dock for some time. I had my own idea of what to expect, and was a little let down when I got a look at the battered vessel. It was much smaller than I visualized, not much bigger than a rowboat. Paint was pealing, the anchor and chain were rusted; the small fishing net came apart when Floyd tried to untangle it. The boat sat low in the water and Pop tinkered with the motor, finally it sputtered to life and we putt-putted out of the harbor on our maiden voyage. The bay was calm as we left the harbor; however, the water became a little choppy as we moved further from shore. Pop was tending to the motor, Floyd sat mid boat and I was in the bow.

About a half-mile out we discovered why the boat had been so cheap. It began slowly filling with water. Floyd looked around and spotted a couple empty coffee cans, obviously there for a reason. He started bailing the water over the side, yelling at me to do the same. Pop turned the boat towards shore. The *Lucky* was filling rapidly, up over our shoes, with no sign of stopping. Floyd and I worked frantically, but it looked like a losing battle.

"Bail faster" Pop shouted. "Here Mary, you take the wheel. Keep us pointed at the shore and I'll bail." About that time the motor sputtered and died. The shore seemed a long distance away. Floyd and I were used to swimming in the Puget Sound and not too worried; however, I had never seen Pop swim and wasn't too sure he could. There were a couple small outboard motor boats some distance ahead, probably trolling for salmon. Pop took off his shirt and stuck it on the end of a fishing rod and waved it wildly overhead.

Floyd's Boy Scout training came in handy. "We got to take off our shoes and tie the laces together. Hang them around your neck, in case we need to swim," he instructed. "That way we won't lose them." The boat was beginning to list to the *starboard* and taking water faster than Pop and Floyd could bail it out. The boat was half full and listing seriously. We were crowded to the *port* side, trying to keep the boat from going under. The whole thing was pretty exciting.

"Let's turn the boat over, before it sinks completely!" Pop barked. We moved over to the *starboard*, which was already under water. I was ready to jump ship and let it sink, but Floyd and Pop leaned over and grabbed the edge of the *port* side and over the boat went; throwing us all in the cold water. Pop came up still holding on to the edge of the boat while Floyd and I treaded water as we bobbed in the waves. "Hang on to the hull, someone will rescue us soon, providing the darn thing floats long enough." My shoes flopped around my neck, but stayed secure.

At water level I could barely make out the trees lining the shore. Treading water I volunteered to swim for help. Floyd said he should go, as he was a stronger swimmer than I was. Pop had crawled up and was sprawled across the hull. As Floyd and I were arguing which one of us should try to make it to shore, Pop yelled, "Be still. I think I hear a motor." He scanned the bay. "I can see one of the fishing boats, and it's headed our way. I guess they had spotted my shirt and realized it was an S.O.S."

The small outboard motor boat came along side with two men in it. After checking to make sure we were all right, the larger of the men threw a towrope to Floyd. He tied the rope to the bow of our overturned boat, using one of his Boy Scout knots. There was only room for one more person in their boat, so Pop hung his legs over the side of our overturned boat and slide off the hull. He dropped awkwardly into their boat. Floyd and I held on the back of *Lucky* and kicked our feet. The two crafts headed slowly back to the pier at Double Bluff where our car was parked.

Pop was very quiet on the way home. "Let me tell your mother in my own way." I felt a little sorry for my dad. Guess we weren't going to be able to fish for sharks this day. It had been a very exciting afternoon and I could hardly wait to tell Bill what he had missed. When we got home I stayed outside cleaning my shoes while Pop explained things to Mom. Bill was real disappointed that he had missed all the fun.

At supper that night I started to tell Bill more about our adventure. "Boy, you should have seen Pop climb up on the hull of the boat," I began.

"Be still Mary Lynn and eat your supper," Pop said stiffly.

"I just want to tell him…"

"Not now Mary, we'll talk about it later," Mom interjected.

"But it was so funny."

Pop jumped up from the table, nearly turning it over. "Can't a man eat his supper in peace and quiet in his own house, without all this jabbering?" He closed the door firmly as he walked out and headed towards the barn. I never heard what Pop did with *Lucky*. However, no one suggested that we go fishing for sharks again. That was over a year ago, and now here comes another surprise.

Bill and I were almost home and I still hadn't guessed what Pop had brought home. "Maybe it's *Lucky* or another boat." No, Bill shook his head. I had one more chance coming before I had to pay up. I had guessed everything I could think of and not even gotten warm. "I give up, what is it? But first tell me what's was so darn funny when I asked you if it was alive?" I asked for the third time.

Laughing again he continued, "Just wait till you see it. Remember you owe me a penny. Come on I'll show you. It's really neat and I can hardly wait to see what Pop is going to use it for." We walked around to the far side of the house and there it sat in its former splendor.

Not really believing what I saw, I was flabbergasted! "Is that the hearse from Hedgecocks' Funeral Home?" Floyd and his friend Skinny Riley had their heads under the hood inspecting the large motor.

"Yep, and ain't it a something? It's a 1933 Studabaker." Bill opened the driver's door and climbed up on the running board and slid in on the leather seat. He honked the horn, turned the steering wheel and made strange motor sounds. The dashboard had a lot instruments and dials. I was afraid to look in the back, in case there was a casket that Pop forgot to leave at the funeral home. The curtain at the window between the cab and the back was royal blue velvet. After checking to make sure there were no caskets, I opened the rear doors. I saw steel guide rails on the carpeted floor. I shivered realizing that was to help slide the caskets in. The windows in back were also covered with worn velvet curtains.

Bill was now out of the cab and had joined Floyd and Skinny checking the motor. As I turned to run in the house to check with my mom, I could hear them taking about pistons, cylinders and horsepower. They seemed completely spellbound over the fact that the thermostat was located in the radiator and was part of the hood ornament.

"What's that hearse doing in our back yard?" I questioned mom. "Did Pop get a job driving for Old Man Hedgecock?" It was the only logical reason I could think of to have a hearse parked at our house.

"Your father has another wild hair. He didn't tell me anything, just showed up early this morning with it. Said he was going to put seats in it and haul workers back and forth to Fort Casey, charging them some ridiculous sum. I don't think anyone will pay to ride to work in a hearse." She sighed and continued snapping pole beans for supper. "But then you know your father! He's like a gopher burrowing through life without seeing all the havoc it causes."

I had mixed feelings. I loved some of the adventures I'd had with Pop and his schemes, but I wasn't sure how my friends would feel about a hearse in our yard. I was at the age where the opinions of my classmates began to bother me. I knew some of the neighbors considered our family "different" and thought my father a little eccentric. Mrs. Stevenson had confided in me that she thought my mother was a saint for putting up with my father's shenanigans. It bothered me when she said that about pop; but then I never liked her anyway.

The hearse sat unmoved in the side yard for a week or so. Pop referred to it by then as the bus. On Friday of the next week I came home from tennis practice and found Bill waiting for me in front of the house. "Come look and see what Pop and Floyd did." Bill liked to be the bearer of news, good and bad, so I never knew what to expect. We walked around the house to where the hearse was parked. "Well, what do you think?"

I was speechless; the beautiful black limo was no longer, it was now painted a bright apple green. Two wooden benches had been installed in the back. The roof was rather low, so it appeared that the passengers would have to crawl on their hands and knees to get in and out. The narrow benches were only about 12 inches off the floor so a man's knees would jackknife up to his chin. Even I could see that it didn't look like a comfortable ride for the 45-minutes it took each way to work and back.

Pop, being forever the optimist, figured that at fifty cents a week for each rider he'd be raking in $12.00 a month. That is, if he could get six of the men to agree to ride with him. Of course he failed to take into account that the hearse got only 4-6 miles a gallon and the worn-out tires needed to be recapped immediately. But never faint-hearted, he was finally ready to begin. He had five passengers the first week, down to three the second and on Sunday his best friend, Ivan, came by to tell him he had found another ride.

"Frankly, Lynn our wives got together and told us we shouldn't be caught dead riding to work in a apple green hearse."

The Game

1939

It was hard to concentrate as Mrs. Spencer droned on about the Magna Charta. History was always one of my favorite subjects, but I had something more important on my mind.

Today was the finals in the Langley School tennis tournament. I was the only seventh grader who had made the finals. I was set to play Mabel *Able* Carr. She was tall, fast on the court, with a powerful serve, and she would have the entire eighth grade to cheer her on. This would be my toughest challenge yet. It had been brought to my attention by my older brother, that Mabel was likely to beat the tar out of me. I had no choice but to play her. I had come this far, winning the last two matches, just as she had, and now we were in the playoff.

I was nine-years-old when I came across a picture of my mother and friends standing on a tennis court, rackets in hand. The men wore black suits with ties. My mother and her girlfriend, Flossie, wore long dark skirts, jackets and high top shoes. This was something new, as I never thought about my mother being a tennis player. I looked closely and seriously at the picture, and took it to my mother for her story about when she played tennis. My mother was a great storyteller and I wasn't disappointed as she described the fun times she and Flossie had playing doubles against all comers in 1916, her senior year at Orange High School, in Southern California.

I had a hard time picturing my prim and proper mother running across a court, to exchange volleys. "I haven't played in years," she said, deep in thought. "I don't think I've had a racket in my hands since your father and I married." Seemed to me that there were a lot of things my mother hadn't done since she got married. I became fascinated with the idea of becoming a tennis player. I watched the high school students as they played, wishing I were one of them. What I needed was a racket. I knew it wasn't likely I could talk my parents into getting me one.

"Money is tight," was my father's stock answer each time I brought up the subject of playing tennis and everything I needed. I dropped a hint or two to my Aunt Katie, who was usually a pushover. We worked out a deal where I would help her with cleaning her house on Saturdays, and she would buy me a racket.

Aunt Katie gave me my racket for Christmas. She had left on the price tag, ninety-eight cents. Several years later following the saga of the aqua formal I figured out that she paid me about ten cents an hour for cleaning her house over a period of two months. Aunt Katie wasn't the pushover I had thought she was.

When spring came, my mom taught me the rudiments of the game, and I was off to set the tennis world on fire. The first thing I discovered was that I had absolutely no natural ability to play tennis. I was awkward, lacked instinct for timing and I tired easily. But I did have determination. Tall and thin, big feet, elbows flapping, I pounded the court, racing after the ball. I played at every opportunity and there were always older, more accomplished players looking for someone to play. Using the side of our barn, I practiced my backhand, and my serve, hour after hour. I gained strength and learned to anticipate my opponent's moves. I began to win some of the games and enjoyed the feel of beating older, more experienced players.

I was in the seventh grade and had just got myself a new racket with money I'd made picking strawberries. I hadn't mentioned to my aunt about needing a new racket as I'd given up my career of house cleaning. So now three years and hundreds of hours of practice later, I knew I was good... but was I ready for Mabel *Able* Carr?

It was two o'clock, time for the big game. Mrs. Spencer frowned as I put my books away and got ready to leave. My classmates grumbled as I left the room. Mrs. Spencer would not allow the rest of the class to skip sixth period to watch any tennis match. I got my racket and hurried out behind the school building to the tennis courts. I was somewhat surprised to see so many kids standing around waiting for the next match to begin. Mr. Willard, the eighth grade teacher, had excused his entire class in support of the tournament. I recognized many of them, including Bunnie Carr, Mabel's younger sister, and her older brother Steve. Several of his high school friends were front and center of the cheering section.

A coin was tossed to determine who would serve first. It was to be a seven game match; the winner would be who ever took four games first. Mabel took the first two games, amid a great deal of cheering. It was looking bad. I rallied and won the next two games.

We had to change ends. Mabel trotted to the net, gracefully lifted her right leg and pushed off with her left foot, waving her racket as she cleared the net. I had never tried jumping over the net, but she made it look easy. The crowd demanded that I do it. After a few seconds hesitation, I ran up to the net and kicked off. I felt weightless, right leg over the net. Eureka! Just as I thought I'd made it, the toe of my left foot caught the net.

I sprawled full length, crashing down on the hard cement. Badly shaken, my wrist, elbow, and both knees were skinned and bleeding. I was mortified as I heard laughing from the spectators. Someone got me a wet towel, and Mr. Willard wanted to postpone the game. I knew if the game were postponed I would not be back. I got up, eyes and wounds smarting, but determined to finish the games. More than that, I knew I was going to win!

The games were tied up two to two. The first player to win two more would be the champion. I served the fifth game and won after a close battle. Mabel served and I lost. Games were now tied, three—all. It was the seventh and the final game. My serve, the pressure was on. I aced the first serve. Fifteen--love; then thirty--love; I had *Able* Mable sweating, but I was bleeding. I double faulted my next serve; the score was now thirty to fifteen; and then a fast return by *Able* was well placed, so that it tied the game at thirty all.

A hush came over the crowd. I clenched the racket as I threw the ball high over my head and slammed my serve into the net. Second serve was right in the pocket. She raced forward and lobbed the ball gently over the net. I was ready and returned the ball just inside the back foul line.

"Nice shot, Mary!" The score was add-in; deuce; add-out; back and forth, deuce; add-in, and finally, game! I was the victor. We shook hands, mingling her sweat and my blood.

As I gathered my sweater and extra tennis balls, I watched as Mabel's friends and classmates crowded around her, talking and laughing. Mr.

Willard congratulated me and told me I'd better go home and take care of my skinned knees. I walked silently towards home, wondering what I'd tell my mother about my torn dress and bloody knees; I began wishing I had a neat nickname like *Able*.

At Coupeville High School, three years later I was one of four girls to go to the Division playoffs held in La Conners. My teammates were Lucy Smith, Frances Wanamaker, and Annie Chapman. I no longer lived close enough to the school to practice daily, and my new interests were beginning to take up a lot of my time. My mother had told me about being in a dance marathon when she worked on Catalina Island. I thought maybe I would enter a jitterbug contest—if I could—find the right partner.

Langley Grade School
<u>Seventh and Eighth Grade Girls Tennis Tournament</u>

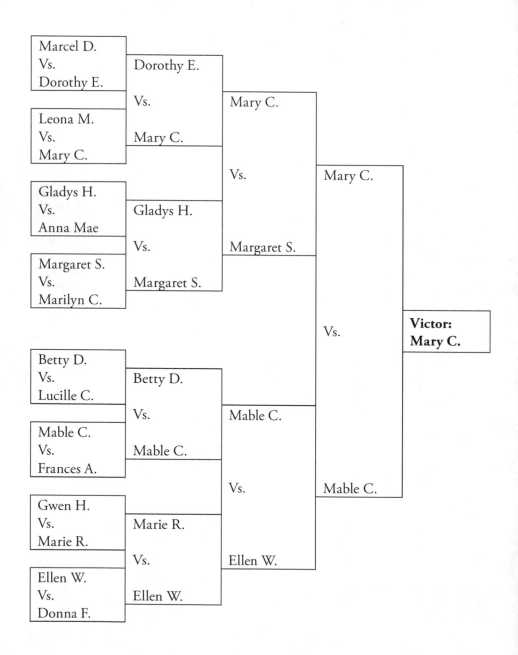

Sex Education: 1939 Style

The drizzling rain began to pick up momentum as we stood trying to decide if we should make a break for home or wait it out on the steps of the school. My family had moved to Whidbey Island, Washington from California a few years before, and my mother still counted the days of continuous rain. She would soon learn it was easier to count the days of sunshine.

I stood close to the three older girls for warmth and pretended I was with them. Forever on the fringe of things, I openly eaves-dropped on their conversation about boys, classes, and Friday's homecoming game. Sylvia, Lucille and Evelyn, freshmen in high school, seemed so glamorous and grownup to my inexperienced twelve years.

With a toss of her long hair, eyes scrunched as if in pain and with lowered voice, Sylvia made a declaration that was the beginning of my SEX EDUCATION. "I sure hate it, but I'm going to be on the rag by Friday. I don't know why it always happens to me!"

On the rag, what does that mean? But wait, there's more! Evelyn, taking a big breath, moved closer and responded, "I know what you mean, carrying around Kotex in your purse, just in case, is really so embarrassing. What if it falls out and some boy sees it?"

I had been quiet up until then and the girls acted as if they had forgotten I was there. But the whispering, references to "the rag" and "Kotex" sent a small electric shock to my brain; making me think this might be something I really needed to know more about. I knew what a rag was; just how you might be on one I had no idea. I thought if given some time I might be able to figure that out, but Kotex was a brand new word. So I did what any inquisitive young woman would do and asked my new friends.

Puffing myself up, trying to look thirteen, instead of barely twelve, I heard myself telling a whopper, "I think I need one, where can I get a Kotex?" I had their attention at last. Lucille got it first and looked at me as if I'd just arrived from Mars rather than California. With the typical superior air of a worldly high school student talking to a seventh grader, she dismissed me with, "You don't know what a Kotex is, do you?"

From the secrecy tone of their voices I knew right away this had something to do with sex! Keeping back the tears of embarrassment, I tried to act unconcerned. Eyes red, head down I stepped out into the downpour. "I got to get home," I shot back, as way of explanation.

Sylvia finally took pity on me. "Why don't you go home and talk to your mother?" So I now had a mission, go home and talk to my mom about SEX. This was so scary; I didn't know anyone who had actually talked to his or her mother about sex.

During the rest of the week I tried several times to bring Kotex up in a causal conversation, but somehow it was not an easy subject to introduce. I practiced it on my dog Buddy, but he didn't seem to know anymore about it than I did. His ears picked up when I ran the "rag" word past him, but then I remembered he had chewed an entire blanket into pieces the size of rags when he was a pup. He may have remembered the excitement when it was discovered.

The relentless rain, from downpour to drizzle, had finally subsided. I found myself alone with my mother, doing dishes on a Saturday morning. My brothers and Pop were in the fields planting the winter squash. *This is it,* I thought, and I decided to seize the moment! Swallowing hard, keeping my eyes on the dishwater and with no warning I blurted out, "Mom, what's Kotex?"

My unsuspecting mother was so startled she nearly dropped the dish she was drying. "Do you mean Kodak?" she finally answered, carefully placing a plate back in the cupboard. Not waiting for my reply, she hurried on, "Kodak is a camera, you know like my old Brownie."

"Oh yeah," I replied with a big sigh of relief, "I forgot." We finished the dishes in comfortable silence, and as I started to leave the house, I decided to finish this sex education once and for all. "Mom, where is our Kodak? I think I'll go take some pictures of my new girl friends, Sylvia and Lucille."

Louise's Revenge

1941

The sound of yelling came from the far end of the football field near a small stand of old fir trees. I could make out the figure of a girl stooping down, picking up rocks and throwing them towards the trees. As each rock was thrown she let loose a stream of choice profanity, the likes I'd rarely heard. She was so intent on what she was doing, she never noticed me. The yelling that first attracted my attention was actually coming from somewhere in the trees. I could make out several boys, my brother included, trying to hide among the branches. I thought that was a good place for them. I had no idea why Floyd and his friends were hiding up in a tree dodging rocks, but I figured they had it coming.

Floyd was a late getting home from school and hurried out to the back yard to finish his chores before supper. "Who was that girl that had you and Chick Goldsmith treed?" I asked trailing after him out to the shed. I stood watching as he chopped kindling for tomorrow's fire.

"She's nobody," he answered, without looking at me, "just some new girl in my class. Her mom and her live in the old Jamison place on Bay View Road."

I dogged on, not satisfied with his answer. "What did you guys do to her to make her mad enough to throw rocks at you?"

"It's none of your beeswax."

I looked at my brother who was three years older than I was and seemed to get away with a lot. "I'm going to tell Mom, and then you'll get it."

"Listen, it was all in fun, so don't say anything, OK?"

I was trying to figure out what I could get if I kept my mouth shut. "Can I ride your bike to school tomorrow?"

"Yea, I guess so," he answered so quickly I was sorry I hadn't asked to ride his bike the whole week.

I soon learned that the new girl's name was Louise Black, and she and her mom had moved to Langley from Bellingham in northern Washington. No one seemed to know much about her, but already there was some gossip about why they moved to the island. My mother carefully explained that I wasn't to have anything to do with Louise. I wanted to tell mom about her throwing rocks at Floyd, but decided to keep it to myself. I thought it might be good for another day on his bike.

While visiting with my aunt, I heard that Mrs. Black was a *loose woman* and was told I should stay away from their place. I was cautioned not to speak to Louise, since the *apple never falls far from the tree*. My Aunt Katie did love good gossip. She always counted the months a couple had been married when she learned they were expecting their first baby. You couldn't get away with much with Aunt Katie always on the lookout for sinners.

Louise was the source of a great deal of speculation. The older boys at school teased her and made up stories of wild parties they had been to, at the Blacks. Most girls avoided her and whispered about her. I wasn't sure why Louise was such an easy target, other than she fought back the best she could. More than once she was called into the principal's office for fighting and once for giving the principal's son a black eye. Still the razzing went on.

She didn't come to school often and I rarely saw her elsewhere in the community. The town of Langley on Whidbey Island was small. Life settled around school, church, county fair and who was going with whom. Louise and her mother stayed close to their home and when she was a freshman she dropped out of school entirely and was rarely seen. Busy with growing up, I seldom thought about Louise as time passed.

It was summer the next time I saw her. School was out and Floyd was taking a bunch of us to Goss Lake, a favorite swimming hole, for the afternoon. Floyd had finally given me his old bike and gotten himself a sporty 1932 Model "A" Ford. Always the wheeler-dealer, he'd take us to the lake if we came up with 18 cents to get a gallon of gas. The kids were all older than I was, but I was included as they needed another nickel that I just happened to have.

As we came to Louise's house, we saw her picking wild blackberries at the side of the road. Someone yelled, "Stop the car!" and Floyd pulled up beside her. Her eyes guarded at first, relaxed a little as Chick asked her if she wanted to go swimming with us.

"I'll ask my mom and get my swimming suit." She turned to go up to the house.

"Yea, right! Forget your suit, save you the trouble of taking it off! I heard you liked to go skinny dipping." The smile turned to tears as she started running across the field, the bucket of berries spilling on the ground. Someone hooted and jokes flew back and forth. I felt sick, but couldn't think of anything to say.

Finally as the car pulled back on the road and everyone was laughing I came out with a wimpy, "Why don't you guys grow up?"

In the fall, when I'd started high school, I'd talked my mom into letting me go to a night football game, which was being held out of town. Dozens of students were packed in the school bus with plenty of chaperones. Students sang the school song while cheerleaders practiced school cheers and flirted with the boys on the football team. The sun had just set and it was turning dark.

Once on the ferry, headed for the mainland, we were told we could to go to the snack bar on the upper deck. As we piled out of the bus, my girl friend, Frances, grabbed my arm and pointed to a small car just ahead. "Isn't that Louise getting out of that car? Who's the old guy with her?"

I could tell it was Louise, and I don't think she noticed the school bus full of her old classmates. We came face to face as we started up the stairs. I could see she had on a lot of makeup and was toddling on new high heels. As recognition came, she started to push past without speaking. I looked at her and back at the car she had just gotten out of. "Are you going to the game?" I asked knowing it was a stupid question, but it was all I could think to say.

"No, we are going to Seattle, and I'm getting married tomorrow. That's my fiancé in the car," she said.

Frances took another look and stammered, "Who is he? He looks kind of old for you."

Louise tossed her long hair and looked defiantly at us. "I don't care; he really loves me, look at this fur jacket he just bought me." I didn't know much about fur, but I was thinking that the rabbit had seen better days.

We stood there, Louise looking like she was trying not to cry. "He's good to me and nobody else gives a damn. I'm going to show all you high and mighty bastards a thing or two."

She didn't look happy and tears welled in her eyes a she turned and walked to the stern of the ferry. I felt funny, like I'd eaten too much fudge, and I started to get back on the bus. I watched as Louise moved closer to the rail, the wind blowing her hair, teetering on those ridiculous heels and clutching the ratty fur jacket. She stood close to the low rail, watching the island grow smaller and smaller. I looked away a second, and suddenly I heard a shout of alarm. She had climbed over the rail and was standing on the very edge of the deck. Then, as I watched, she slipped or pushed herself away from the rail and slid into the dark cold water.

"Man over board! Man over board!" Chaos everywhere! People were running and shouting; others were asking what was going on. The driver of the car, the man Louise said she was going to marry, was trying to throw a rope into the swirling water. I saw him start to climb over the rail, but he was held back by one of the crew. The captain unaware of the drama on the deck below, the ferry churned ahead, until it came to a sudden standstill. A lifeboat was lowered and several of the crew wearing life vests climbed in and pulled away in the darkness. Later a Coast Guard Cutter joined the search. Flashing lights and surreal sounds traveled over the water then grew distant as the minutes past.

The ferry returned to the island dock. The game was canceled and many of the kids from the bus were questioned. Someone had told them that they had seen Louise talking with me. I was taken aside and asked what Louise had said to me. I was so scared I could hardly remember what we actually had talked about. "She just told me she was getting married." I wanted to tell them that she really didn't sound happy, but then I may only have imagined it.

The offical looked at me real hard. "Mary, did you see how the accident happened?"

"Not really," I replied afraid to meet his stare. "Oh there was one thing I think I saw…"

Impatiently, "Well, what was that?"

"I'm not sure, but I think just before she went overboard I saw her look back at the bus and raise her hand in a small salute."

"Why in God's name would she do that?"

I thought I knew, but didn't have any idea whom I could tell.

A fishing boat found her body the next day, and rumor had it that her shoes were missing. The little fur jacket she had on constricted her arms and probably weighed her down. The official ruling was that she had slipped and it was a tragic accident. My Aunt Katie wanted to know if she was pregnant. I cried a lot, but after all, I hardly knew her. I didn't go to the funeral. I had a bad cold. The paper said the funeral had one of the largest turnouts ever! Yes, Louise, you really showed us bastards.

The View from the Outhouse

1943

While I was growing up we were never fortunate enough to live in a home with indoor plumbing; outhouses were still quite common in rural areas. During the winter I dreaded having to go out in the cold and rain, baring my skinny behind to the elements. The wind whipped through the cracks in the boards and created an updraft, keeping visits short. Always an unpleasant smell greeted the visitor and was most noticeable in the summer months. Having grown up with outhouses I didn't give them much thought until after one embarrassing afternoon when I was about fourteen. I promised myself that when I got my own home I'd have a real bathroom.

Outhouses came in many sizes and styles. There was the standard privy for one, for one adult and one child, or the large economy size with two adult seats for the couple that liked to do things together. Some people attached *store bought* toilet seats for comfort. For obvious reasons the location of the outhouse needed to be moved often and kept downwind from the house.

When I was in my early teens we lived in a remote part of Whidbey Island surrounded by woods. Our nearest neighbors were several miles away and often many days would go by without having any visitors or seeing anyone other than my own family. I was home alone one day and needed to use the facilities. Our outhouse was set off by itself, near the path that led down to our own little lake. It was a beautiful fall day and since I was absolutely alone I left the door open so I could see the lake and take advantage of the fresh air.

I was studying an old Sears and Roebuck catalog that just happened to be handy, and daydreaming about how I could impress the cute boy at school if I had some new clothes. Glancing up I was surprised to glimpse two hunters walking up the hill from the lake. My surprise quickly turned to horror as I realized my predicament. The large door to the outhouse stood wide open and swung outward. My panties were down around my ankles and my skirt spread out across my lap. There was nowhere to hide!

As the hunters rounded the curve I became in full view. The man in front looked up and our eyes met. He stopped short and the man following ran into him, nearly knocking both of them down. I'm not sure who was the most surprised and embarrassed. I shut my eyes briefly and sat perfectly still. If I couldn't see them, maybe they wouldn't notice me. They started to turn, but decided the damage was done and I could hear them continuing up the path. It all happened so fast, and I'm not sure why, but as they came abreast of the open door I greeted each of them with a squeaky "Hi."

Each in return bobbed his head and responded with a friendly "hello," eyes straight ahead, never slowing.

I never saw them again, thank goodness, nor did I find out who they were. I can only imagine how their hunting stories would include one about how they once trapped a young blond in the outhouse! When I told my parents, my father couldn't stop laughing and my brothers teased me about it often.

Several years following this embarrassing incident, I went to work during the summer for a very wealthy family in Seattle. I had my own room and bathroom. Although I was impressed by the size and beauty of the house, my first letter home went into great detail about the eight bathrooms!

My Secret

1943

The summer before I turned sixteen I was caught trying to shoplift a dress from The Bon Marche' in downtown Seattle. This is one of my darkest secrets, and I have never told a living soul before. The only three people who knew at the time were the woman security guard who caught me, the head of security with whom I made a bargain, and me, the guilty little thief. I imagine the security people never thought about me after the incident and are now long gone as they were middle aged at the time. I have read that the only way three people can keep a secret is if two of them are dead.

For as far back as I can remember it was expected that I would not only do my share of work at home, but I would find seasonal jobs in the summer. From the time I was nine years of age it was expected that I save the money I made, working in the fields each year, to buy most of my school clothes. I usually picked berries, cherries, cleaned the neighbor's chicken house and pulled mustard from the alfalfa fields. There would be about thirty dollars when it was time to buy my clothes for school. My folks didn't make me work, but if I wanted any thing extra I needed to come up with the money. This was not unusual at this time, for in the 1930's and 40's most of the kids I grew up with contributed to the family income.

The summer between my sophomore and junior year of high school I persuaded my parents to let me go to Seattle and find a job that was more to my taste than picking berries. I described to my mother how I would earn a great deal of money and then be able to buy all my clothes and even bring some home for Christmas. I could be very persuasive and even though they were not convinced that it was a good idea I brought in my big gun. My friend, Jo Ann Grisswalt was going and would be staying with her grandmother and wanted me to be her roommate. What we neglected to tell them was that her grandmother was only willing to let us stay with her for a couple weeks; we then had to find a place of our own.

It was the middle of WWII and jobs were plentiful even for inexperienced fifteen year olds. I needed to get my Social Security card and for that I needed my birth certificate. When it arrived I found out that my name, which I had always believed was Mary Lynn Chase, was in reality Audrey Jean Chase. My parents acted confused over this discovery and argued about how it happened. They decided it was one of life's little mysteries. I decided that I really was adopted; a thought that often obsessed me when ever I was in trouble.

Once in Seattle I quickly found a job at the lunch counter in one of Bartels Drug Stores. I was now a waitress, but a very inexperienced one. The pay was thirty-five cents an hour, plus a meal. For you the reader, I have to explain that Seattle, during the 1940's was a *port* town and was overflowing with sailors, either returning from sea duty, or getting ready to ship out. Fort Lewis, the temporary home of young soldiers newly drafted, was just a few miles away. The times were frantic, creating a carnival-like atmosphere. I was not particularly popular at school and was just beginning to date. But all of a sudden here I was, on my own away from home for the first time, with thousands of homesick boys.

Nearly every evening, Jo Ann and I made our way to the Trianon Ballroom and danced until it was closing time. When we were not at the dance hall, we took in all the wonderful movies or roller-skated. The next morning I dragged myself to work, promising myself that tonight I'd go home right after work and get a good night's sleep. By the time my shift was over, Jo Ann and I changed clothes and headed for another night on the town. We spent our small wages as fast as we were paid. I missed at least one day a week for I often overslept from lack of sleep. I was not a good employee, but help was hard to come by with the lure of big wages at Boeings and other defense plants. I was too young to get a job in any defense plant. As bad as I was at my job, Bartels and I were stuck with each other.

I learned one of the most valuable lessons in life while I was working there. One day my feet were hurting, and the lunchroom was crowded. I was tired from staying out late the night before. I had mixed up my orders, while several people stood waiting to pay their bill. The manager was watching me and didn't look happy. One of the customers, a nice looking middle-aged man, motioned me over to where he sat. He leaned forward and looked right at me.

Very softly he said, "Young lady, if I hated my job as much as you obviously hate yours, I'd find something else to do, even if it paid less." I was stunned. I had no idea that my attitude was so obvious and reflected on how I treated my customers. That lesson has stayed with me my entire life and I have used the same tactic with people whom I supervised that were in the wrong field.

When for the third time Grandma Grisswalt asked us to please find a place of our own, we rented a nice room with a family. The place came with bathroom and kitchen privileges for five dollars a week. We seldom used the kitchen, choosing instead to eat hamburgers and cokes. I had never been on my own before and had absolutely no discipline.

The summer passed quickly and it was almost time to return home and to school. I had written my folks several times describing my job and how great things were going. But as I took stock I realized I hadn't bought any new clothes and I would be returning empty handed. So this would mean I'd start my junior year at Coupeville High with last year's wardrobe. More than any thing I needed a coat, shoes and a couple of dresses, making do with my worn and tattered underwear. What was worse, my mother would know that once again I had broken my word and fouled up big time. I refused to think about what I should do; I was running out of time.

I was staying at the YWCA, as we had given up our room and Jo Ann had already returned to the island. I had one more day of work and what little I had coming would pay for my room at the Y, a ticket for the bus trip home and a couple extra dollars that I'd probably eat up. With no money for a movie and no one to go with I was passing time wandering through the upscale Bon Marche' Department Store.

I always loved the smell and sounds of large department stores although I could not afford their prices. I thought the sales ladies in their black dresses, high heels, and sleek hair-dos were quite elegant. I was just looking around and for the first time found the bargain basement. The clothes were on sale and if I had any money the basement would have been a good place to shop. I looked at some dresses and decided to try them on, even if I wasn't buying. I took three to the dressing room fantasizing which one I would wear on the first day of school. I was not planning anything I just was killing time. I looked out the curtain of the dressing room and no one seemed to be paying any attention to me.

The dress I was trying on was a light blue, my favorite color, long sleeves and with hidden buttons down the front. It seemed to be made for me. I looked again at the sales lady busy with another customer. I slipped my skirt over the dress and pulled on my red sloppy-joe sweater. In the mirror I looked kind of fat and lumpy, but not too bad.

Head down I walked out of the dressing room, rode up the escalator, with my heart pounding and I was beginning to sweat. Looking neither left nor right I made straight for the exit. I stepped out onto the sidewalk feeling a sudden rush, thinking that I'd made it. I hurried to get as far away from the store as I could without running. Just as I started to cross the street I felt a firm hand slide into the crock of my arm. In confusion, I looked over and here was this nicely dressed lady holding tightly to my arm. *What the…?*

"Just keep walking, no one will notice anything," she quietly instructed. "They will just think we are mother and daughter out shopping."

I thought about making a break for it, she must have felt me tensing up. "Don't even think about it," her voice firm.

Gone was sweet mommy, replaced by a cop. I wondered if she would shoot me if I made a break for it. We kept on walking, pretty mother and daughter out for a nice afternoon. An idea came to me…this solved one problem; I would not need any school clothes in jail. I pictured going to the police station, where I would be booked. I thought about my one phone call and wondered who I would call since my folks didn't have a telephone. My parents would probably notice I wasn't at home when school started.

My new companion and I walked along arm in arm and finally entered a business building. *It doesn't look like a police station.* I thought as we took an elevator to the second floor. Two doors down we stepped into a small office then moved into a small dressing area next to the restroom. I was told to take off my skirt and sloppy-joe sweater.

I tried to feign surprise as we both looked at the blue dress I had on with the store tags still attached. "How in the world…" I began.

She just shook her head as I tried to look as if I had never seen it before. "Take it off and get dressed," was all she said.

Once more dressed in my own clothes we went into the inner office. A large man sat alone at a desk and we took a seat in front of him. Instead of yelling at me or hitting me with a rubber hose he spoke to me in a soft conspiring way. I soon confessed how I'd taken the dress. He seemed so kind and understanding that I wanted to confess all my other sins of the summer…*missing work, not writing my mother every week and spending all my money on movies and dances.*

He gave me a serious talking to, and of course I swore I would never do such a thing again. As soon as he said I could go, I hurried to the Y to pick up my belongings and caught the evening bus home to Whidbey Island.

Mom did not question me about the lack of a new wardrobe, nor did she sympathize when the rains started and I had to wear last year's jacket. I decided that next year I would stay home and pick berries, or get a job in the brush plant. I probably was not ready for the big city.

The Problem with Shoes

April 1946

During my childhood, on one of the first warm days in spring, an epidemic would break out. If you listened you could hear children all over the country begging for the same thing. It started with one or two of the older kids deciding it was the time to take off their shoes and go barefoot.

"Let's do it!" "Are you going to do it?" and finally, "I have to ask my mom first." Then began the race home, slamming the screen door and finding mom in the kitchen. "Please, please," I often begged, "can I go barefoot? All the kids are doing it."

Sometimes I got permission and other times my mom would just shake her head. "It's too soon, Mary, you'll have to wait until it warms up." I could always tell if the answer was final or it was worth another try. Outside, the other kids would be waiting, shoes intact. It was amazing how the mothers seemed to agree without ever talking to each other.

When it was finally time to go barefoot and I had permission to take off my shoes, I was overcome with a sense of freedom. I loved the feel of running barefoot across warm grass on early summer mornings. When the orchard was irrigated my brother and I walked through the almond trees and delight in the feel of warm mud squishing between our toes. I think that is how the idea of the modern spa was born.

On the down side, I had forgotten how my tender feet stumbled on rough pebbles and felt the sting of stubbed toes. By the end of the second week my feet toughened up so I could run over the hot pavement, or walk through puncture vines with the best of them. During the long warm summer months, shoes were suffered only for special occasions and church on Sunday. The last of August was time to think about putting shoes on again and going back to school.

Getting new shoes was a big deal and very exciting. I often wanted the first pair I tried on, no matter how tight they were, afraid that my mother would change her mind. This led to serious problems. By the end of the month my poor toes would be cramped; and I'd hobble painfully along, not daring to complain.

Throughout grade school my brothers and I each got one new pair of shoes, which were expected to last the entire year. A single pair of shoes a year led to serious problems—mostly that our feet kept growing at an alarming rate. My brother Bill was a terror on shoes. Two weeks into the new school year and his shoes were ready for the trash heap. Some years, his feet grew so much he wore the shoes out from the inside, toes poking holes in the sides and out the ends of the shoes.

One year we drove to the mainland and went to Sears and Roebuck for new shoes. The salesman instructed me to stick one foot inside an apparatus, which looked somewhat like a standing scales, and then push the button. What a keen experience--I could see the bones of my toes squished against the sides of my shoe. I later learned this was called a fluoroscope, first cousin to the x-ray.

I was a big kid and my feet grew in proportion, meaning they were large. The local Star Store, where normally we bought our clothes, carried women's shoes to size eight only. When I finally discovered that the Chandlers Shoe Store in Seattle stocked women shoes to size ten, it was one of the highlights of my life.

As a young adult I loved to wear high heels, and often wore shoes with two and a half inch heels. I liked the way they made my legs look, long and sleek. As I began to get older I started buying shoes with two inches heels. Then I found that shoes with one and three quarters inch heels were more comfortable—you get the picture. At last safety became an issue. By the time I retired, I was in the sensible one and half inch dress shoe. From there it was all down hill, and today as you can see, flats are *in*. The only choice for me now is shoes with heels lower than the toes, which will probably make me walk like a duck.

Leather shoes were rationed in the later years of WWII, and for several years following. The shoe industry came up with an answer for the shortage of leather shoes for civilians. These were made from pressed cardboard tops and composition soles; the leather normally used in making shoes was reserved for the military. It was late 1945, and I was living and working in San Diego when I first heard about these shoes one could buy without using a ration stamp. I needed a new pair of shoes and thought I'd give it a try. I found these neat wedgies, cardboard tops, open toed, and sling back heels, and dyed a beautiful *Midnight Blue*. They looked rather stylish, and from a distance I didn't think anyone would notice they were actually made of cardboard.

I was getting ready to wear them for the first time. The occasion was a semi-formal dinner being held at the beautiful Grant Hotel, in honor of a group of Naval airman, just returned from the south Pacific. My roommate's boyfriend was among the honored guests. Between the two of them they had set up a blind date for me with one of his buddies. I had asked only that he was to be tall and that he like to dance.

Daisy and I had planned this occasion for several weeks and were dressed to the nines! The day dawned wet and windy. The song, *It Never Rains in Southern California*, was written for San Diego, but contrary to the song, it had rained hard all day, pounding the streets and flooding the gutters. We took a cab from our apartment to the hotel in the center of downtown. Pulling up to the curb I stepped quickly out of the cab...into the gutter, both feet ankle deep in water. By the time we got to the grand lobby where our dates were waiting, I realized that with every step my shoes were squishing and leaving little puddles of Midnight Blue.

Daisy spotted her boyfriend and with him was a tall good-looking naval officer. As my blind date, Bob, and I were introduced, I looked down and saw that my new wedgies were beginning to come apart, much the way the inner roll of toilet paper would if it got very wet. When we finally were seated I hid my feet under the table the best I could. During the dinner my shoes continued to unravel, and I wasn't sure how I was going to make my escape. The evening didn't go very well, and when the music started Bob wanted to dance. I had better sense.

I was worried how I would make it out the door when it was time to leave. I decided to take the high road and ignore the fact that my shoes were coming apart. With head held high I made straight for the exit, deaf to the slapping sounds of wet cardboard on the marble floor. As we stood curbside saying our goodbyes, I took one last look and pretended I didn't notice the trail of cast-off pieces from my shoes. Bob promised to call, but we both knew he was just being polite.

Crescent City Redwoods

1954 - 1956

Gone, but Not Forgotten

1954-1955

"Daddy's home! Daddy's Home!" Christy announced importantly, and rushed outside to be the first to greet him. Three-year old Betty trailed after her and stood back watching eagerly as my husband, Woody, pulled up to the house. With baby Paul in my arms, I stepped to the window and smiled at the familiar scene; daddy arriving home from work, being greeted by his "girls." Sharon, our oldest at seven and a half, was at the table just finishing her homework.

Today was a special day, for Woody was bringing home our new car. There it was, and it was a beauty. We had been without a car for sometime and had been using the old work pickup for all transportation. It was getting a little crowded with four growing children and a fifth one on the way.

The shiny red and black 1953 two-door Hudson, with all the latest bells and whistles, was beyond anything I'd hoped for. I had admired the Hudson cars since I was a teenager. A girlfriend of mine dated a navy pilot who had a 1941 Hornet, dark green with a flashy hornet decal painted on the hood. How classy can you get? My brother-in-law, John, was a "Hudson man" and had a new car every other year.

In the 1950's Hudson was one of the original companies that offered two and then three colors on many of their models. The body of our car was a deep blood red and the top was shiny black with black leather interior. It was less than two years old with only 20,000 miles on it. The test drive, with windows down, so the girls could wave at friends, was a total success. Dinner was late that evening.

At this time we lived in Fort Dick, a little town outside Crescent City. My husband had a small "gypo" logging company and currently was doing selective logging in the redwood grove to make way for the now famous Redwood Highway leading into Crescent City from the south. He and his partner, Carl, employed only a few men, doing most of the falling and bucking themselves.

I enjoyed being a stay-at-home wife and mother. Typical for most of the families we knew, the husbands worked in the woods and the wives cared for the home and children. I was expecting my fifth child in early spring. Needless to say, our children were all beautiful and exceptionally bright. After all, this is my story.

We planned a vacation in August to Whidbey Island. My parents still lived in the house on the lake property. Following a brief failed marriage in Oregon, I moved back with my two baby daughters. Woody had come to Whidbey in 1946 with a job offer, and immediately fell in love with the beauty of the island and the endless hunting and fishing opportunities. Two of his brothers, John and Byron, and their families soon followed.

Sharon was three and Christy two when Woody and I married and moved to the Oregon coast. Betty, our third daughter was born the next year in McMinnville, Oregon. We were soon on the move again following the logging boom to Northern California. Paul entered the world in a hurry while we were living at Big Lagoon, California. When Woody got the contract to log the redwoods, we moved to Del Norte County. We had been gone from our beloved island for over four years and this would be the first time we could make the trip back.

The kids were excited about seeing their grandparents and assorted cousins. The two-day drive was without incidence and we made a snappy entrance arriving in our shiny Hudson. We were enjoying our short stay when on the third day Woody began complaining of severe internal pain. It continued to worsen. Not wanting to spoil our vacation, he refused to see a local doctor protesting he would be ok.

Woody Mills, 1954

By the next morning he admitted he needed to get home. I had never heard him complain before and could not remember him ever being sick. I knew it was serious. Regretfully, we cut our visit short and headed for California. Woody sat hunched over, clutching his side, I drove nonstop, except for gas and food, until we reached home. Once back in Fort Dick he went to the doctor and our wonderful life started to unravel.

He was treated for an ulcer, and when a strict diet failed to bring any relief he went back for further tests. The doctor decided to do exploratory surgery and found a mass on his pancreas. Remember, this was 1954, long before modern technology. The surgery site was closed, and I was told there was nothing more they could do. Later when I pushed for more details it was explained to me that he probably would not live beyond a few months.

I couldn't believe it. He was young and strong, and I had never seen him sick before, not even with the flu. By now he was weak from the surgery and the pain was persistent, food didn't interest him. I brought him home for one afternoon on Betty's fourth birthday for cake and ice cream. It was the last time he would leave the hospital. The children missed him and kept asking when Daddy was coming home.

Our house was about twelve miles from Seaside Hospital in Crescent City where Woody was being treated. I use the word "treated" lightly. It appeared there was no treatment other than occasional pain medication. It was 1954 and was the era of guarded use of opiates for fear that the patient would become addicted. I visited him every day bring the children, however he could barely tolerate their chatter due to his pain. It was better to wait and see how he was before bringing them to his bedside.

Woody had stopped eating and became emancipated and eventually developing a horrible pressure sore that never healed. Days ran into weeks and then into months. The doctors never told him the truth and Woody still half believed that he could get well. I, too, was a coward and went along with the game of "when I get over this", "when you come home."

Christmas came and went with little fanfare. There was no income; I had to give up the house and we were allowed to rent it back. We finally had to apply for welfare. In the meantime I was juggling the visits to the hospital, school for Sharon and Christy, caring for Betty and Paul and getting ready to have another baby in February. I was profoundly depressed and gained unwanted weight. In late December I developed a series of boils under my arms and on my buttocks. I was a physical and mental mess.

Days passed in a blur. I took care of each day, hour by hour and would not let myself think about what tomorrow might bring. I felt I had lost all control and was existing in a vacuum waiting for something—someone— to make things right again. The girls had stopped asking when their dad was coming home. I gathered my sweet babies close and they seemed to sense my loneliness. Many times I would wake in the morning to find a tangle of little arms and legs snuggled in beside me. During the night one by one they would crawl out of their beds and make their way to find comfort in my big bed.

Woody wanted to see his mother. His parents lived in Maryland and I had met them only once, a few years before, when they came to the west coast and spent time with their assorted grown children living here. I got to know Mother Mills and she taught me how to make the best biscuits this side of the Mississippi. One day over coffee she told me about the loss of her oldest son, Ebert, due to a freak accident while he was working in the shipyard in Baltimore. Tears filled her eyes as she described how he was taken so suddenly and she never had a chance to say goodbye.

So it was with confidence I wrote and explained the seriousness of her son's illness and his desire to see her. She wrote back that it wasn't a good time as they were putting a new roof on the barn, so couldn't really afford the trip. I realized that she must not have understood what I was saying. Using a pay phone, I called her to better explain how sick Woody really was. Her answer was the same, new roof, not feeling very well so she just couldn't come at this time.

I tried one more time saying, "Mrs. Mills," not mother "I don't think you understand, Woody is dying and he wants to see you."

"I'll pray for him, but I can't come," she said.

Angrily I reminded her how she had sat at my kitchen table, tears in her eyes, agonizing over not being able to say goodbye to Ebert. I finished with "I'm giving you the opportunity to say goodbye to your son, Woodrow."

She stayed firm but promised once again to pray. When I told him his mother was not able to come just now he didn't act surprised and just turned his head to the wall.

Janice was born at Crescent City Seaside hospital on a rainy Sunday afternoon, but we had a little excitement first. I had checked in the night before and things were not progressing very fast. I shared the labor room with another mother-to-be whose delivery was long over due.

It was during the quiet afternoon visiting hours when my roommate's water suddenly broke and it was action time. I never knew where all the nurses had disappeared to, but there was no response to our frantic calls.

After announcing that her water had broken, she started screaming, "It's coming! The baby is coming!" Her husband ran from the room looking for a nurse, a doctor, but would have settled for the janitor. In the midst of labor myself, I lumbered out of bed not sure what to do, but went over to her bedside.

She grabbed my hands and hung on "Don't leave, don't leave me," she pleaded. "Oh God, it's coming out right now." She was right. It happened so quickly I had little opportunity to think what I could do.

Always full of advice I clung to the bedrail and offered my best, "Whatever you do don't push! Breath through your mouth and pant."

It was then she let out a loud shriek through gritted teeth and pushed. The baby's head began to emerge. All my experience having babies of my own kicked in. "Good girl, pant, pant. Now one more push."

She pushed. By then we were both laughing and crying. I started to reach down for the baby, but my own pain hit and I doubled over. The room was suddenly filled with hospital personnel. As a nurse helped me back in bed she demanded to know what I thought I was doing. She scolded me as if the whole thing was my fault. I didn't have time to explain as I had more important things to do. Janice, at seven and half pounds arrived a couple hours later.

By this time Woody had been moved to the county infirmary, another name for nursing home. Someone arranged for him to be brought to the hospital in an ambulance to see us the day after Janice was born. That was the only time that he saw his youngest daughter. His time was running out.

So now there were five little ones, Sharon, Christy, Betty, Paul and Janice. After all the excitement of a new baby and my mother visiting, we were back to the same routine. A few times I would pile all of us in the Hudson and we would go for a ride up along the Smith River and end up in the state park. I clung to the car as the only thing that made us still like other families; the one means of independence that I still possessed.

Two weeks before he died we had a long talk. I could tell he had been preparing himself for this and had finally accepted the fact that he was not going to get well. He knew he was going to die soon. We talked about the children. He wanted to take care of us and made me promise some things that I knew I probably would not do. He told me that he loved the family and was sorry he would not be there to help the kids grow up. I had not kept him informed of how destitute we really were. He thought that things were about the same at home. "You have the house and you have the car," he almost smiled when he spoke of the car, "so you should be OK there. Sell my truck to Carl, he always wanted it." Carl, his partner, had bought the pickup just before Christmas, and that money, too, was gone.

Woody's final two weeks he drifted in and out of consciousness, often hallucinating and talking to people not there. At one point he thought his mother and father were in the room next to his and he was positive they had visited him earlier that day. I didn't try to convince him otherwise. By Wednesday of that week his breathing was labored and raspy, and he could no longer speak. Saturday evening I was alone with him in his room when I suddenly realize he had stopped breathing. As I summoned the nurses I waited for them to do something.

I waited…nothing! Gently the nurse said, "Why don't you wait in the side room next to the nurses station, the doctor will be here soon and he will want to talk to you." I did as I was told.

Woody had asked to be buried on the island; his brother, Byron, contacted the local funeral home and arrangements were made. My husband took his last train ride to Seattle, where his coffin was picked up and driven to the island. My mother, three oldest girls and I rode with Irma, my sister-in-law and her husband, John, to Washington.

Byron told me that they were waiting to hear from his mother to schedule the funeral. "They are flying out from the east coast in the next day or two." He explained. I couldn't believe what I was hearing and then I completely lost it.

"They are not coming to his funeral; I absolutely will not have them." I was crying and trying to explain.

Byron, forever the peacemaker, was the family spokesperson. "Mary," he began, "These are his parents and of course they want to be here. It wouldn't look right if they didn't come."

For once I would not give in. "I gave them the opportunity to see him when he was alive. I begged them to come. I wrote and then I called them, explaining how sick he was and how much Woody really wanted to see them. They were too busy. Now they want to come because it wouldn't look right not to?!"

I was yelling and didn't care; my mother was trying to calm me down. I shook off her restraining hand and continued in a deadly calm voice. "If they try to come to the funeral, I'll call the police and have them thrown out. I'm his wife and I have the final say about who can and who cannot come."

I had no idea if I could do that or not, but the threat seemed real enough. I never knew what Byron told them, but they didn't show. They sent $80.00 to help with expenses. I told Byron to put it in the pot. Needless to say, years later, when their will, well over a million dollars from sale of their dairy farm, was probated, Woody's children were not included.

Following the funeral I took stock of my situation. I was twenty-seven years old, a high school graduate with no special work skills, a mother of five children eight years of age and under, and owing my brother-in-law eleven hundred dollars for funeral expenses and no visible means to pay him back. Things looked bleak. I wasn't sure just how, but somehow we would make it. So began another chapter in my life.

It's Only a Car

December 1955

Seven months after the death of my husband, Woody, I was still looking for a decent job. My sister-in-law offered us temporary use of their guesthouse in Eureka while I looked for work. I drove down in my 1953 Hudson Sedan to look the situation over, taking Betty and Paul with me. I had left the two older girls and the baby with a friend and intended to be back the next day.

It had been raining hard all week, and I hadn't had any luck job-hunting. Thinking things over, I decided that I didn't want to live in my relative's back yard, and we needed to get back to Smith River where we were staying with friends. The kids had adopted a young cat that had wandered into my sister-in-law's yard and it was making the trip with us. I had the back seat loaded with clothes and personal items that had been stored, so the car was full.

We left at noon, plenty of time to drive the hundred miles and get home by dark. It was raining so hard I had the windshield wiper at full speed, and even then visibility was poor. Highway 101 followed along the rugged northern California coast. At times I could see the swirling water of the Pacific Ocean directly below. The storm never let up and the stiff wind made it hard to keep the car on the road. Betty and Paul were happy to be going home and excited about owning a new pet. I had to concentrate on the road and my driving. I thanked the *powers that be* that there was not much traffic, and the logging trucks, which usually were a hazard, were missing. The winter storms had shut down logging operations until next spring.

The cat had finally settled down and Paul had dozed off. He was such a sweet baby, my only son. I thought how Woody would have enjoyed teaching him to hunt, fish and all those boy things. I sighed. We had passed the town of Orrick, and climbed to the ridge where even in good weather the road was dangerously close to the edge of the cliff. As we approached the summit, Betty told me about what she had learned in Sunday school the previous Sunday. Far below I could see the road twisting down the mountainside and at the bottom was the raging Klamath River. Across the bridge was the small settlement of Klamath.

The town had one main street, with several business buildings, a grocery store, at least two bars and the café that served as the Greyhound bus station. A garage, a chain saw repair shop and a service station were further up the street. Homes dotted the land near the river as it followed the side of the mountain. The highway went through the middle of the town and then continued on to Crescent City. I was becoming worried; it was after three o'clock and getting darker. I would need to hurry to make it home before total darkness. I tried to remember if I had ever seen it rain this hard for so long a period of time without a break.

When the car topped the summit I felt a lurch and a grinding sound as rubber and rim came together. I groaned...a flat tire! I berated myself for not having a spare. I stood looking down at the offending tire, and quickly became soaked with my hair was plastered to my head. I knew I had to get help, but was undecided about what I should do. It was nearly a half of mile to the bottom of the hill and then across the bridge into town. I couldn't leave the kids in the car, but hated to think about dragging them out into the storm. I was still trying to decide my course of action, when an old beat up pick-up pulled alongside. Two men, obviously loggers from their dress and hauling a chainsaw in back, were inside the truck.

The driver got out of the truck and came over to see what my problem was. "Where's the spare? We can put it on for you."

"I don't have a spare...."

In a moment a second man got out of the truck and glanced at the car and then looked at me closely. He squinted in the rain and looked back at the red Hudson. "Aren't you Woody Mills' wife?"

I nodded and he continued, "I heard about him being sick and all. I'm sorry. Woody was a hell of a good man. He was the best damn logger I ever did see." He took a step closer and looked in the car at the kids huddled together on the front seat.

"I'm Lucky Rainwater, and I worked with him a couple years back."

I felt better, we were now with friends, and they would help me. We discussed several options; but they didn't think much of my suggestion that they go into Klamath and get me a new tire. Both were anxious to get home out of the storm. It was finally decided the children and I would ride with the driver, and Lucky would try to drive my car down the hill, flat tire and all, to the garage in Klamath. I could get a new tire and I could be on my way.

We piled in the truck with the driver and Lucky climbed in my car. He slowly edged the car down the road with us following slowly. We crossed the bridge over the swollen river and up the street to the garage only to find a big "Closed" sign on the office door. We left the car parked in front and drove back to the café to find out why the garage was closed. The café was full of people sitting and standing around talking loudly.

Lucky asked one of the men near the door about the garage. "Haven't you heard? There are flood warnings. Everyone is trying to get out of town to higher ground," he said.

The waitress spoke up and told us that the sheriff had called; and they were sending a bus to take those without transportation to Crescent City. My two new friends were anxious to get to their homes and see about their families. I assured them I would be safe at the cafe and would wait to be evacuated with the others. I thanked them for their help and they were relieved that I was someone else's problem.

The children and I had a sandwich and something to drink. With so many people crowded in the small building and anxiety rising with passing time, the air was charged with excitement. People were friendly, so Paul and Betty with their cat were the center of attention. The tension mounted as darkness fell, the pounding rain continued, and still no sign of the bus.

Joe, a local Indian who had been taking small parties across the inlet in his jeep, came back to report he could no longer get out that way. Several huge trees had fallen across the highway to the north. Trying to call out, about the expected bus, the waitress found the telephone dead. Shortly after, the lights went out. We sat in stunned silence. Betty hugged my arm and Paul climbed into my lap. Flashlights helped someone find a few candles and then a lantern was lit.

A small group decided to try to walk back out over the bridge; they knew if they made it to the far side, it would be a fourteen-mile walk to Orrick. They soon turned back. The river was raging and the cement bridge was creaking and swaying dangerously. We were cut off from the outside world. Old timers talked about earlier floods and prophesied that when the ocean tide crested, the whole town, including the café, would be under water.

The door burst open and the driver of the jeep came tumbling in sopping wet and wild-eyed. "The dam is gone. The dam is overflowing! The bridge is coming down," he screamed against the howling wind.

Chaos! Panic! People were moving this way and that. We could hear the roar start to build far up the mountain. The building shook; people screamed and pushed their way from one door to another. But where could they go?

Someone, a big man trying to get folks' attention, but unable to be heard above the roar of the water and the frightened cries of those trapped in the café, jumped on the counter and took command. He finally fired off the rifle that had never left his arms.

"Let's get on the roof; it's our only chance," he ordered as he grabbed a stool and put it on the counter. I looked up and saw a trap door that probably led to the attic. "Wait right where you are while I figure out if we can get to the roof from the crawl space."

All eyes watched as his legs disappeared through the trap door. I noticed that he pulled his rifle in after him. I decided to do exactly as he told us. A minute or two passed and his head reappeared. He asked for a couple of volunteers. Two men who had been standing in the back stepped forward and jumped on the counter where he helped pull them up into the crawl space.

We heard some banging and a small crash that sounded like glass breaking. The man with the rifle dropped back down on the counter. Pointing at a nearby man and his son, he explained what we were going to do.

"Now, you men will stand next to the counter and we'll get everyone up here, one at a time. Billy is in the attic and will help everyone out the side window and up on the roof where Herb will be waiting."

Two teen-aged girls and their mother went first. It was soon my turn. I went up first, looking down so the children could see my face. I reached down for Paul and gave him to Billy who was standing beside me. Finally I leaned down and pulled Betty up, still clinging to the thoroughly traumatized kitten.

To get to the roof I would have to climb through the broken window and stand on a small ledge. I was to reach up to where Herb would help pull me onto the roof. "I can't do it! I'll fall." The ledge was narrow and the flooding street was a twelve-foot drop below. The noise from the raging river was deafening and we had to yell to be heard over the howling wind.

"You have to get on the roof and this is the only way. You don't want your kids left here do you?" That finally did it. I started through the window and nearly panicked. I knew I had to do it.

"Hang on to the top of the window frame and step on the ledge. Look, part way up, we made a toehold in the side of the building where we knocked out some of the wood. For God sakes don't look down. I'll hold your legs…you won't fall." Herb leaned over the edge of the roof ready to help.

Out on the ledge, I reached up and Herb grasped my hands, steadying me as I lifted my foot and found the toehold. With unbelievable strength, he pulled while I pushed myself up and over the edge. I lay in the freezing rain, shaking from fright and efforts of my climb.

Billy came out the window and stood on the ledge; reaching in he got Paul and held him up to Herb who handed him to me. Betty and her kitten came next. One by one each of the others were pushed, pulled or crawled onto the roof. I've often thought about those men who surely saved many lives that day, and I wondered where Herb and the others found the strength to get twenty-one adults and five small children up through the crawl space and out the window onto the roof.

After the initial feeling of relief that we made it this far, we looked around. Our clothes were soaking wet and the wind stung our eyes. It was after 9 p.m. and pitch dark. The only lights were from lanterns here and there. The roar of the flooding river and rising tide made conversation difficult. We could see dark water, full of tree branches and other debris, spilling out of the river and filling the street below us. An old man sitting near the children kept a running commentary about past floods, and the rising tide.

"Tonight the tide is to crest at 10:10 P.M., I keep track of all tides, as I once made my living fishing and once I get a habit it stays with me." He didn't need to explain to me what a tide crest was; being from Whidbey

Island I, understood. I held the kids close, wondering if the building could stand any more pressure from the raging current. We heard the bridge give way, so now the only hope of escape was to the north.

Betty looked towards the garage and whispered in my ear "Look Mom," she pointed up the street. Someone had hung a lantern on an eave of the garage and we could just make out part of a red and black car. "That's our car. All my clothes and dolls are in the back seat."

"I know honey," hugging her closer.

"Are my dolls going to get wet and drown?"

"Oh honey, I hope not." But I wondered if "we" were going to get wet and drown.

Suddenly it felt like a horrible earthquake; we could see a bank of water like a small tidal wave rushing up the street towards us. Several nearby buildings crumbled and pieces of their wreckage were being carried past us out to sea. Someone handed me a rope and I tied it around the each of the kid's waist and the other end around mine. Whatever happened I wanted us to be together.

We held on to each other and I could hear some people crying, others screaming and a few praying. I silently blamed Woody for dying and leaving me in this mess. The small grocery store next door collapsed and started to break up. A large piece of the storefront banged into our building but our refuge continued to hold firm. A dead cow floated by on its way out to sea. It was hard to believe the battered cafe could last much longer.

It was nearly 2 A.M. when I realized the rain had stopped and the current had slowed. The tide had crested at 10:10 P.M. and was now receding, taking most of the town of Klamath with it. Miraculously, our little building still stood and we had all survived, wet, cold and shaken, but alive. We heard a motor and could make out the light of a small boat coming down the middle of what had been the main-street. Several people stood in the boat using a searchlight looking for survivors. We all shouted and wildly waved. A man using a bullhorn told us to hang on; help was coming. We were giddy with relief. The old fisherman, who had stayed at my side throughout the entire night, said he had thought he was a goner this time, for sure.

"I wouldn't have minded for myself so much as I'm an old man, but I'd hate to see any of the little children hurt."

"Me too!" I thought, "And now he'll have a great story to tell next time he and his cronies get together."

We waited several hours, chilled to the bone but relieved that the initial danger had passed. Daylight was beginning to break when I heard someone shout, "Here it comes!" A tug-boat, normally used to tow logs down the river to the sawmill, came chugging straight up Main Street. The water was about fifteen feet deep and the tug pulled up to the building. We were lowered, one by one, to waiting arms and a given a dry blanket against the chill.

About a third of us were on the first trip up the street to where the water met the road. Rescuers were waiting to help. There would be a short walk and climb over the fallen trees that blocked the road. We needed to avoid the electric lines that were still down and presumed live. The long overdue bus and cars were waiting to take us into Crescent City.

As I stood on the deck of the tug thinking how lucky we were to be alive, I could see the havoc the storm had caused. It was now a new day and it appeared that the sun was going to come out. I hoped that no lives had been lost. I could see that all the homes along the riverbank were under water. The town had been destroyed, but I hoped it would be rebuilt.

I looked towards the sea and saw all the debris piled up along the beach. There…it couldn't be…but it was, my Hudson, half submerged with the front end pointed towards the ocean. As I watched, it gave a shudder and the front end rose up as if a giant hand was lifting it and then dropped it back down to disappear under water.

"That's my car, that's my car!" I cried out. Irrationally, I felt as if I needed to rescue it. It was a major link to our former life, so carefully planned for us by Woody. I grabbed the arm of one of our rescuers. "You don't understand," I shouted in his face, "That's my car!"

"Lady, get a hold of yourself; you and your children are safe. It's only a car."

Once on dry land I began walking to the safety of the bus I started crying. I hadn't been able to cry since the first weeks of Woody's long illness. Even when we lost our home and went through his funeral, I was dry-eyed. I hadn't cried last night through all the danger. But finally, the sight of my shiny red Hudson, with our personal belongings, disappearing into the water was just too much. I started to weep and I was unable to stop. I sank into the wet grass at the side of the road and wept until there were no more tears.

La Grange, California

1957 - 1960

Moving Up

December 1957

The children and I had moved into the old government housing project in Rodeo, near Richmond, California, after I injured my back. I had been working for Kerr's Industrial Catering for six months. I was in a great deal of pain even following several months of rehab and unable to work. That meant we were back on welfare. It was the lowest of low times to date. But we were all together. Sharon was now in the fifth grade, Christy in the third and Bets was a first grader. Paul four and Janice three years of age were still at home.

Pop had come to spend the holidays with us. Two days before Christmas someone broke into our unit while we were all at the movies. Coming home late I quickly put the children to bed and Pop and I retired soon after. The children woke me early the next morning with the devastating news that all the presents that had been under the tree had been opened and most of them were missing. The brightly colored Christmas wrappings were torn and scattered about the small living room. Sharon and Christy found what was left of the Christmas gifts in the outdoor incinerator next to our building. The model of the Russian Sputnik, a school project that Sharon had made, some new clothes, a pair of skates, two little dolls, hair ribbons and a few toys were in the incinerator burnt beyond use.

A little neighbor boy, who lived directly below, confessed that he and 13-year-old brother had come in through the kitchen window. They had taken the presents, opened them and then not knowing what to do, put them in the incinerator hoping to destroy the evidence. The mother cried when I confronted the older boy in her presence. She pleaded with me not to report the break-in to the police as the boy was already on probation. She was sorry, but she had no money to replace the damaged presents. I thought about calling the police, and now think that I should have. I knew the gifts would not be replaced and felt sorry for the boys' mother. The following week he came running up the stairs chasing one of the girls. I was still so upset I pushed him and he tumbled down the stairs. He got up, uninjured thank goodness, but my blinding anger frightened me. I had to find another place for us to live.

In February, at my dad's suggestion, I borrowed a car from an acquaintance and we all went to visit my Great Uncle Art. He and Great Aunt Rose lived in the little town of La Grange in the Mother Lode about 35 miles east of Modesto. Uncle Art was my mother's uncle, brother to my grandma Lula Newcomb. Art and Rose had spent most of their married life in the hills above Mariposa mining for gold.

Great Uncle Art spent nearly 25 years looking for the elusive pot of gold. They had barely eked out an existence and had finally given up the chase. Weary of the lonely, rough life they moved to La Grange and built a small house when he turned 65. They were now on the county payroll and settled in for the long haul. I remembered them vaguely from my childhood and looked forward to the trip.

Pop had called ahead to let them know we would be visiting. They seldom had visitors so were excited about our visit. We arrived in early afternoon amid much fanfare and hugs all around. A grand tour was in order to see the town they loved and called home. There really was not much to see.

The town consisted of a short street with a small grocery store, IOOF Hall, Luvagi's Bar, Vic's Garage, Keeler's Gas Station, U.S. Post Office, and The Corner Café. A few homes were scattered along the main street. At the top of the hill over looking the town was the Catholic Church, graveyard and the public grade school.

La Grange was built on the high banks of the Tuolumne River with an old the bridge leading north to Don Pedro Dam and on to Sonora. Just off Highway 132, leading east towards Coulterville, stood the rodeo grounds, famous for having the first rodeo in the area each year. Hundreds of cowboys and rodeo fans swarmed to La Grange for the wild two-day event each spring. Alcohol flowed freely and turned the quiet hamlet into a rowdy frontier town for the weekend.

During the gold rush years it was a bustling mining town with hundreds of miners and Chinese Coolies living and working the minefields. There were miles of secret dark tunnels beneath the town and long forgotten artifacts from that era still can be found. The town slowly died and became nearly deserted after the gold rush was over. Not quite a ghost town since a few families hung on and began to prosper running cattle over the brown hills. The town itself barely made a wide place in the road.

La Grange came to life again briefly in the late 1940's. A huge earth-churning dredger tore up hundreds of acres of the riverbed, blighting the landscape and disturbing the natural habitat of spawning salmon, looking for the last of the gold. By the time we visited in 1958, there were less than a hundred souls to call La Grange home. In addition to a few old timers, there were four or five cowboys working on nearby cattle ranches, six or seven older widows and a couple of stray families who had just got caught short passing through, and never made it out. The medium age was close to sixty

After living and working in Oakland, the sleepy hamlet seemed like a God sent. The kids immediately fell in love with the town and the river. Uncle Art knew of a small two-bedroom house for rent across the street from the Corner Café. A short phone call and by five o'clock it was ours for $20.00 dollars a month. Everyone was happy, Uncle Art to have family close by, and my father and I were anxious to get my family out of the housing project in Rodeo. What was intended as a brief visit to La Grange became our home for the next three years.

We never discussed the fact that I had no car, very little furniture and, knew no one other than Uncle Art. Nor did I face the obvious truth that I was probably one of the very few single persons under 50 years of age within a 30-mile radius. However, hope springs eternal; so with a light heart and without a backward glace we loaded our belongings and what little furniture we had, moved into our new home, and into the beginning of the La Grange years.

Bittersweet Days

1958-1960

We had no more moved into our new little home in La Grange when Pop once again came to visit. During his brief visit the grocery store went up for lease. It was a typical mom and pop county store with everything from canned goods, commodities, fresh fruit and vegetables, to sundries and fishing tackle. The store was made for them, and after mom came for a look they took possession immediately, moving into the small quarters in the rear. Pop had finally found his calling. He took great pride in running his own business and quickly settled into life in a small town.

The children loved having grandma and grandpa just down the street. Sharon spent most of her free time "helping" grandpa run the store. Everyday, one by one, the children visited the grocery to spend time with their grandparents. The kids probably ate up a lot of the profit.

Sharon, Christy and Betty started school in the county schoolhouse—all eight grades in one room with one teacher. The first year we lived in La Grange there were twenty-three students in the entire school. Sharon had four classmates in the fifth grade, but some grades had only one child. It must have been challenging for the teacher, Mrs. Mansey, to try to engage all of the students in any meaningful learning. I discovered that Betty, in the first grade, spent most of her time with color crayons and a coloring book. She got an "A" for coloring within the lines. The four or five older boys in the upper grades came and went as they chose, and were disruptive during class time. They were the terror of the younger children and the teacher. The following year there was a new teacher, Mr. Elick, who changed the school for the better.

We were not used to the heat of the central valley and summer hit us with a vengeance by the middle of April. The Tuolumne River was our haven and we spent hours swimming and playing in the cool waters of our own pool. A small beach on the far side of the bridge became our playground. In the middle of the river there were several partially submerged lava rocks. The kids named the largest one, Blackie. It was a milestone when one by one each of the children swam well enough to dog paddle out to Blackie, where I would be waiting and then back to shore.

Our Family in La Grange

The walk to the river was straight down a long hill that, of course, made the walk home straight up. Often we would take our lunch or dinner and spend the entire day. The first time Sharon lugged a ripe watermelon down the hill and left it cooling in the waters, no one had thought to bring a knife. No problem, it was placed on a beach towel and I smashed it with a rock. We all dug in, hands and faces soon covered with melon, but a quick dunk back in the river took care of that.

The children thrived and had the run of town. Janice, at three and a half, loved to walk by herself to grandpa's store, a distance of about two blocks. She would stop first at "Uncle Harry's" gas station and visit with Harry and Tess. Next stop was Vic's garage where she was greeted by Angie, Manual and Vic, if he wasn't too busy working on someone's car. At the garage, she could pretty well count on a Tootsie Roll that would hold her until she arrived at the store. Unfortunately, Janice preferred the middle of the street for her travels, which was a big concern for all of us. I finally assigned Paul to watch out for her, which he took seriously for the next 15 years.

Paul and Janice Mills

The salmon ran during spawning season in the river, and there was a slue up by the water tanks that had catfish and fresh water perch. We discovered a special fishing hole west of town off the highway to Snelling. A series of deep potholes made during the 1940's quest for gold, and now fed by underground springs, had the best fishing in the county. The huge dredger was moored at the water's edge in its final resting place, as it had nowhere else to go.

GOLD DREDGER AT LAGRANGE, CALIFORNIA   J-123

The Dredger

To reach the ponds we borrowed the key to open and relock several cattle gates and then we drove about half a mile on a seldom used and bumpy road. Once there we found that it was worth all our trouble, and were rewarded by a good catch of freshwater perch and a refreshing swim in the warm waters.

On our first trip to the site, we had brought live minnows in a bucket to use for bait. While we were settling in our chosen site on the deck of the dredger, my mother was getting her pole ready for her first cast when she looked down just in time to see the last minnow spilling out of the bucket into the waters below.

"Janice, what are you doing?" Mom cried out.

"I can see little fish down there," she told her grandmother. "I think ours would be happier swimming with them than in this little bucket." It seemed reasonable to her four-year-old thinking.

"That was our bait, foolish child! I can't believe you dumped them all."

After everyone calmed down, Pop went to the truck and got a small shovel and dug some worms. Mom kept the can of worms close by her side. The sun came out and we caught a nice string of large perch.

Mom and Pop with their catch

A larger house next to my folks' store became vacant and we quickly moved into it. This older two-bedroom home had a big screened in sleeping porch. I rated the master bedroom, Christine, Betty and Janice shared the second bedroom, and Sharon staked out the sleeping porch. Paul, being the only boy, had never had a room of his own. When we moved into the new house he found a large walk-in closet off the hall between the living room and kitchen and claimed it as his! The room, about 8' x 8', would accommodate his bed if it were placed on an angle; a nice little retreat from his four sisters.

The house was heated by a wood burning stove in the living room, and I had ordered a cord of oak for the winter. Borrowing my dad's red pickup, and taking Betty and Janice with me, I left Paul in Sharon's care, and went to pick up the wood. Paul's interest in fishing and his natural tendency to do things for himself added one of our more colorful memories. As the story goes, Sharon went next door to play a game of gin rummy with her grandpa, and Paul decided this was a good time to replenish his sinker supply. He had watched an older neighbor boy make sinkers by melting lead and carefully pouring it into holes drilled in an old tree stump to harden. The process with hot molten lead could be very dangerous and I would never have allowed Paul to do it by himself.

When I finally made it home with my pickup full of oak, I pulled down the alley to unload the wood in our back yard. I immediately saw black smoke billowing out from the screened-in back porch. Ordering the girls to stay in the cab of the truck, I made a dash up the back stairs and in the door. The black smoke burned my eyes; it was coming from the cellar door, which opened onto the screened-in back porch.

Without thinking it through, I hooked up an old hose to the faucet at the stationary sink and turned the water on full blast. Water spurted out in all directions from holes in the rotten hose and I suddenly remembered why it was laying in the corner. I was soaking wet by then, but undaunted, I undid the hose and grabbed the dishpan from the kitchen and filled the pan with water. I started for the cellar door only to trip on the hose I'd left laying on the floor, further drenching myself. By then the smoke was clearing. I refilled the dishpan and carefully climbed down the cellar steps.

At the bottom of the stairs there was a little pile of smothering twigs and pieces of partially blackened wood. Nearby was an old coffee can filled with pieces of lead along with the metal eyes used to make sinkers. I made sure the fire was out and climbed slowly out of the cellar. I looked through the house; I knew that Christine was at her friend, Judy's house, I guessed that Sharon was with her grandparents, and Betty and Janice were with me. That left Paul. First things first, I unloaded the oak firewood and returned the truck to my pop's garage and took the key into the store, Betty and Janice trailing after me.

"My God, Mary," exclaimed Mom, looking at my wet and sooty clothes, "what ever happened to you?"

I let Betty tell the story how I had heroically put out the fire. I decided to go home and clean up, before I went looking for my little fisherman. As I finished my shower there was a knock on the front door. Bobby Cole, who lived with his mother at the hotel, which had recently opened, had come on a mission. "Mrs. Mills," Bobby began, "Paul asked me to come and tell you he wants to spend the night in a tree."

"And what tree is that?"

"You know...the big tree in back of Zona Simpson's house. Paul wants me to bring him a cover, a pillow and, oh yeah, two peanut butter sandwiches; he says he's hungry."

Bobby was about ten years old and saw nothing unusual in a six year old planning on spending the night in a tree. "I'll take care of Paul and thank you for letting me know where he is." I slowly closed the door and began to see the humor of my clumsy attempts to put out the twig fire, especially when I realized that the cellar walls and floor were completely made of cement. However I needed to have a straight talk with my son.

I casually walked over to Zona's backyard. Seven-year-old Dale Hook met me about half way and let me know that Paul was in a tree and was hungry. I walked around under the big tree to give Paul some time to decide his next move before I called up to him.

"Hi Paul," I called out softy, "It's time for supper. I want you to come down from the tree now."

Paul looked down from the second fork in the big tree. "I want to sleep here tonight. I told Bobby to tell you." He peered through the branches and asked hopefully, "Did you bring my peanut butter sandwiches?"

I finally convinced him he should come down and we could both go home and have something to eat. Finally realizing that it was unlikely that I was going to send up sandwiches and bedding, he started down the tree. Half way down he stopped and looked down at me.

"Mom, if you smell smoke on me it's 'cause Zona has been burning trash and some of the smoke might have gotten on my clothes." How can you stay angry at that kind of creative thinking? The next day his grandfather helped him make some real neat sinkers.

As I got older, however, I lacked for adult companionship. Briefly, a young divorced woman with three children the same ages as my three youngest lived down the road. We became friends and even when she moved away we stayed in touch for 20 years. Another single woman with two boys moved in for a short time; tragedy struck when she died in a single car crash on a mountain road. Days passed pleasantly, but after the children were in bed at night I would feel utterly alone and unhappy with my situation. I remember going out one Friday evening around 10:00 P.M. and looking up and down the street for some sign of activity. I felt adrift and imagined that this would be the way a castaway on a desert island might feel and maybe I was really the last person on earth. Try as I might I was unable to visualize how I could make changes that would make things better. I spent some time fanaticizing and there was usually a tall dark stranger, somewhere, ready to rescue the children and me.

Change did come and it came suddenly. My father died without warning one April morning in 1960 of a heart attack. This left a big hole in all our lives. I helped my mom in the store occasionally and life continued. My mother continued to run the store until her retirement in 1963.

The short years at La Grange provided many wonderful childhood memories for the children. For me, it was like the eye of the storm, a short reprieve from the real world. It was a difficult decision to leave, but I needed to find work. So with mixed feelings, that summer we moved to Modesto and a new chapter in our lives began.

Sharon was ready for high school and Christy would be going into the seventh grade. We got into the housing project on Robertson Road, a move that I regretted almost immediately; however, that is another story.

La Grange has changed since we lived there. By the 1970's, many of the old-timers were gone; houses and businesses were taken over by outsiders living the "hippy" lifestyle. It wasn't long before the town took on a neglected appearance. Finally in the late 1980's, the dredger company made good their promise of rehabilitating the land and riverbed disturbed in the 1940's during the last quest for gold. The town, river area and land surrounding La Grange were declared a historical landmark with state and federal money available to clean the town up. Christine, Janice, Paul, his daughter Amy, and I went to a reunion for those who had attended the school at one time or the other. It was a bittersweet day for me.

Today, La Grange city limits reach out many miles and the population has grown. Families, looking for a saner way of life, much as I was nearly 50 years ago, are moving to the available land, building homes and living the good life.

Modesto, California

1960 - 1969

The Light

1961-1962

When I first met the angel, I was working at the little coffee shop behind the Greyhound Bus Station and my five children and I were living in the two bedroom rental on Virginia Street in Modesto. I didn't recognize her as an angel when she first started coming into Sally's Café, sometime in the fall of 1961.

I had worked at Web's Drive-In previously, but heard that the cannery paid much better. So in June I tried to get on at Tri-Valley Cannery by standing in the parking lot at shift change, hoping to get hired. I did this around the clock without any luck for over a week. Men were always the first to get hired and then the floor lady would point to three or four lucky women. I never figured out how it was decided who would be picked and finally gave up in despair. So here I was back as a fry cook and waiting tables.

As I walked home from work one blustery October afternoon I realized it was my birthday. I sighed; I was feeling a bit sorry for myself. Here I was, another year older and no better off than I'd been six years ago when I first became a widow. It was getting harder and harder to meet expenses working for minimum wage. Approaching the house, my spirits lifted as I saw my mother's car in the driveway. Smiling I thought, "Mom, never forgets."

Opening the front door I was greeted with "Happy Birthday, to you, Happy Birthday, Dear Mom," completely off key. Waiting for me were all five kids and my mother smiling in the background. A strong smell of garlic dominated the small dining room as I surveyed the table set for supper.

Everyone was talking at once. Paul waited his turn then said, "Sharon made me butter the bread." A large greasy smear on his shirt validated his claim. Janice, the youngest, was quick to blurt out, "I got to help frost the cake."

"That was suppose to be a secret, blabber mouth," admonished nine-year old Betty, "Anyway, I did most of it."

Christy, clearly in charge, announced that supper was ready and we all sat down to heaping plates of spaghetti, green salad and of course, the garlic bread. I started to thank my mother. "I had nothing to do with it." She explained, "Sharon called and invited me. The kids did it all. Only thing I brought is the ice cream."

It was soon time for the main feature. Christy and Betty brought in the lopsided cake with pink, yellow and green frosting. "We used all the food coloring in the cupboard. Pretty wild, huh?"

My concern was whether the cake would make it to the table before the top layer slide off the platter. "There are only thirteen candles, that's all we could find," Paul piped up, "Sharon said you wouldn't notice."

"That's true. Anyway," Sharon added, "you wouldn't be able to see the cake with all those candles on it."

"Make a wish, make a wish, Mom, and blow out the candles." Everyone clapped as I did just that.

"I hope you wished for a car." Sharon said wistfully.

"I'll bet you wished for a handsome boyfriend," giggled Janice.

"Or at least a rich one," added Betty.

"She can't tell, or the wish won't come true," Christy said. "Isn't that right, Mom?"

"That's right Christy, I can't tell."

As I was drifting off to sleep later that night I thought about my wish. It was the same as it had been for the last six years. "I need a decent job so I can support my family. There has to be something that I can do to change our lives." Even as hard as I tried to make my wish come true, I went about each day without much hope that it would.

At Sally's Coffee Shop, like most small eating establishments, we had our regulars, so I noticed when an attractive dark haired young woman started coming in several times a week. She would arrive around one-thirty after the lunch crowd had cleared and order a cup of black coffee. A tall good-looking man in jeans and boots, whom I presumed was her boyfriend, would join her. I overheard their conversation and learned he was a long distance truck driver and ended his run about the time she had to go to work. Sometimes she would wait and he would not come in before she had to leave. At those times we would chat while she sat quietly waiting. She seemed interested in hearing about my children and once revealed that she had always hoped to have a boy and a girl.

"I always planned on having a family, but now it's too late. I've settled on being the *favorite aunt* to some of my friend's kids."

One day she surprised me by asking me what I thought of her boyfriend. "He's a hunk!" I admitted. "But I really don't know him that well."

I had no intention of saying that I thought he was a big flirt when she wasn't around. By this time we were on a first name basis, and Karen continued to come in two or three afternoons a week. I noticed that the boyfriend came in less and less…the romance was cooling.

I was under the impression that she had chosen this café for their afternoon rendezvous, due to its proximity to the truck stop where he parked his truck. I now know that was not the reason. The real reason had to do with her *special assignment*. She actually came to see me, to evaluate my worthiness to receive divine intervention. Angel's are busy I understand, and they must very carefully screen all applicants asking for help.

Karen was always dressed for work in a white uniform, white hose with white shoes, which led me to assume that she was a nurse. When I asked about her uniform she told me that she wasn't a nurse, but actually a Psychiatric Technician and worked at Modesto State Hospital. I didn't know what a Psychiatric Technician was, but it sounded important and I was impressed. I had never considered the state hospital as a possible place of employment.

"A Psychiatric Technician," she explained, "provides care to people who are mentally ill and unable to take care of themselves. I just transferred here from a much larger place." She studied her cold coffee. "You know," she said quickly, as the door open and her boyfriend came in, "not everyone is suited for that kind of work. It takes a special kind of person. Lots of people quit."

I thought about what she said the next time we had a chance to talk. "So how does the hospital recruit new Psychiatric Technicians, if there is a big turnover?"

"Well," she started, looking at me very carefully, "they have their own training program, and trainees are paid while going to class." I sucked in my breath as I threw some hamburger patties on the grill for the teenagers who had just placed their order. I was anxious to hear more and find out what the catch was.

"The only catch is that it can be hard work." Karen explained. "You know, you really ought to apply, you'd be so good at it. I can tell you like working with people. The pay is not a lot at first, but there are great benefits."

It sounded so good, but I still was still skeptical. "I don't have a college degree," I told her at last.

"You don't need one, the state provides a 12 months' training program and all you need is a high school diploma and pass the entrance and physical exams." I felt a stirring deep inside, and she must have seen it on my face for she continued to urge me to put in my application.

Karen seemed deep in thought as she closed her eyes for a moment. "In fact," she said smiling brightly, "they are taking applications this week. Go out and see about it." As I carried the French Fries and hamburgers over to the teenagers huddled around the little jukebox attached to the back wall of the booth, I thought about what she had told me. Walking back to the counter, I glanced over at Karen. I was startled to see a soft flickering light behind her dark head. It had been raining all day so I looked out the window to see if the sun had finally come out.

My mom drove me out to the hospital administration building the next day to see about putting in an application. I was immediately scheduled for the next test. The office clerk who was taking my application was a little confused when she checked to see when the next written exam was scheduled.

"I'm surprised about this schedule. I was under the impression the next test wasn't until March. But this just came in yesterday afternoon, and it seems that we are now scheduling one for the fourth of January." Frowning, she looked again at the exam notice. "You just made the deadline. If you had been a day later you would have had to wait until March."

Did I just hear the soft fluttering of wings? I wondered to myself.

The holidays passed and I found myself with about fifty other candidates in the old Officers and Nurses Club, ready to take the state exam. A large woman, who told us she was from Sacramento, seemed to be in charge. There were four or five proctors circling the room. It was explained to the group of hopefuls that once the test started, no one would be allowed to leave the room. We were cautioned about talking to one another. "Start when I tell you," instructed the woman in charge, "and you will have an hour and a half to finish."

I finally ran out of time, sure that I had failed miserably and glad that I had not quit my job at the coffee shop. Six weeks later I received a letter scheduling me for a personal interview and a physical exam. I was going to make it! I needed to get some cute white uniforms and white shoes; I was almost a nurse!

Twenty-six new trainees and I started April 23, 1962 and had a one-day over-all orientation. Part of this orientation was a tour of several carefully chosen wards housing patients. I'm sure it was part of the *let's weed them out before we waste anymore time.* The theory was if you show up the next day you were a keeper. The tour was not pleasant, and you were introduced to life in an insane asylum at its very worse.

At the end of the day we were each given a large skeleton key and our ward assignment. We were to report to our ward the following morning to work a few hours and attend class for the rest of the day. We had no idea what to expect or what was in store for us. I was handed a key and told to report to D-17, I asked the instructor what patients were there. "I have no idea, but you'll find out tomorrow," was his standard answer for all who asked about their assignment. "I will tell you that D row is closed officially for patient housing, but D-17 is being used temporary while the regular ward is being painted."

That evening my kids were excited to hear about my new job. I got wound up talking about everything I saw and heard that day, so I had a hard time going to sleep. I was very apprehensive and I wondered what I had gotten myself into this time. There was a big knot in my belly the next day as I parked my mother's car in the back near D Row.

I walked along the quiet corridor, looking for D-17 without seeing another soul. As I stood in front of the door, I took several deep breaths, trying to calm my heart palpitations. I took out the large skeleton key and reached up to unlock the door. My hands were shaking and my fingers were icy. I tried several times to get the key in the hole and when I finally thought I had it, I dropped the key on the floor.

For one mad moment I thought, "Hell, I don't need a job this bad."

Staring at the door of D-17, the key once again in my hand, I looked around trying to decide what I should do when I noticed two individuals coming down the long corridor. The light from the outside door was behind them so I could just make out two silhouettes. With the lengthening shadows spreading in front of them, it looked as if they were floating down the corridor. I stood and waited as they drew closer, and then saw that it was a man and a woman in white uniforms.

They stopped as they came up to me and the man spoke first, "What's the matter? Key won't open the door?"

As I nodded to him I glanced at the dark-haired woman standing beside him. She smiled at me. "Karen!" was all I could say before he opened the door with my key. Handing it back to me he gently pushed me in the ward, then closed and locked the door from outside.

And that is the true story of how I started my career in nursing.

Smile and the Whole World Smiles with You

August 1962

My life settled around studying and working with the patients at Modesto State Hospital, as a Psychiatric Technician Trainee. I had found something that was truly exciting, and I looked forward to going to work everyday. I studied hard and took special pains to do my very best at work. I spent half of each day in class and the rest of the day on the ward. Things were good at home and the children were busy with school and friends.

I found it rewarding to work with the chronically mentally ill patients, many who had been institutionalized for twenty or more years. In the early 1960's, it wasn't unusual for a person, having once been admitted to a state hospital, to remain there for the rest of his or her life. Psychotropic medications, which eventually changed the whole treatment of mental illness, were just being developed. However, the patients, in the back wards at Modesto State Hospital, were simply being warehoused, as there was no place for them to go. Whatever symptoms and behaviors had been present when they were first hospitalized were long diminished and the patient was a shell of his former self.

I was shocked when I first saw a staff member slap a woman patient who wasn't moving fast enough to suit her. Not all, but many Technicians used physical force to control the patients. I was upset to see this abuse and talked about it to my classmates. The general opinion was. *Don't ask.*

Don't tell. As trainees we were warned that *what happened on the ward stayed there.* It sounded like a veiled threat when I was told of others who had reported wrong doings and were ostracized so completely that they usually left.

On my third assignment, I found that the Technician in charge and her sidekick disliked and mistreated the patients both physically and mentally. Accidentally, I discovered that they were also stealing from them. They, and probably in cahoots with the man who ran the canteen, had developed a scam. This is how I figured it worked. Many of the patients had income from Social Security and some had private assets that were deposited in the hospital trust office. The trust officer would issue canteen scripts monthly, which the patient could then spend at the canteen for personal items, or the staff could purchase needed items for them. The canteen books were usually kept locked in the office for safekeeping.

On this particular ward, the sidekick would take the script to the canteen and buy personal items and snacks. I saw her push a grocery cart, loaded with new purchases into the office, where she locked them in a large locker.

Several times I offered to pass the treats out to the patients, but I was told they would take care of it. In the first month I never saw any of the treats given out. The beginning of the next month once again the sidekick left with the books and brought back the cart full of new purchases. She unloaded the cart and everything was squirreled away in the locker. I offered to pass out candy bars or sodas to the patients, and again I was told they would do it later. Some of the items were personal care items, such as shampoo, deodorant and hand lotion. The patients never had an opportunity to use the purchases, instead only soap and shampoo issued by the state was utilized.

I was in the office one day to get a chart and the door to the locker was ajar. The shelves were empty and yet only a week before, I had seen a cartload of goodies and personal items being placed in the locker.

I needed to tell someone about my suspicion, but whom could I trust? I thought about the stories I'd heard of others who had broken the code of *what happens here, stays here.* It was a clear warning not to carry tales. But I decided that this, and the treatment of several of the ladies, was so serious that I could not over look it. Normally I would have gone to the supervisor, but the supervisor covering this program was a special friend of the Charge and the two went to lunch together fairly often. I decided to tell one of my instructors and ask his advice.

I made an appointment for the following day with Mr. Dana. He was not happy with hearing about potential abuse and shocked to hear about the stealing of the patient's funds. "What are they doing with all the stuff they buy at the canteen?"

"I'm not altogether sure, but I think they take it back to the canteen and the manager resells it and then they split the profit." Mr. Dana didn't look convinced, so I hurried on. "At first I thought they were taking it home for their own use, but there's no way they could use everything they buy. I just know they buy a lot of stuff, the patients never see it, and then it is all gone."

"You know, Mary, you have really opened a can of worms; if it gets out that you reported this, you will be run out of the hospital. Old timers (Bug-Houser's) stick together and you won't be welcome on any ward." Mr. Dana looked like he might cry, I'm sure he didn't want any part of it. "It is up to you, Mary, what ever you decide to do, remember the chain of command, and do it right."

I met with the supervisor the next day. She sat, stoned faced, as she listened to my complaint. I did not know if she believed me or not, but I could see she was becoming angry. Whether she was angry with me for telling her, or angry about what had occurred, she never said. She quickly dismissed me and said she would take care of the situation. As I left her office she looked at me, "Mrs. Mills, you are not to tell a single soul about our conversation. Is that clear?"

The next day when I reported to work, the supervisor met me and told me I was being reassigned to a new ward in a different program. "I think you will be happier working on a different type of ward. This is not to be considered retaliation for reporting something you thought you saw. But, I think you probably now realize you were mistaken." I just stood and looked at her, hardly believing what I was hearing.

She looked at some papers that were scattered on her desk as she continued. "So, I have decided a transfer is the best for all concerned.

My mind in turmoil, I slowly nodded agreement. It hit me that I could either accept the transfer, or I could quit the program. My future depended on my decision. Thinking back to that incident, I believe it was at that very moment that I made a resolution that stayed with me for my entire career. It was apparent that changes had to be made to a system that allowed such blatant mistreatment of one group of individuals by others. If the employees, who were paid to be responsible, condoned abuse, or at the very least turned their heads, what could be done?

I had risked losing my job and/or being labeled a troublemaker, and seemingly no one cared that patients were being abused. I decided that when, not if, I was in charge, I could help bring about the changes that were needed to protect those who could not protect themselves. I came to realize that changes could only be made from within the system. If I didn't like what I knew was going on, I could either quit or get myself into a position of authority. To start, I vowed that I would never stand by and see another staff person abuse one more patient regardless of the personal cost.

Taking the note that she had given me I saw I was now assigned to B-6 and made my way down the long corridor. Mr. Cole, was who was in charge, met me at the door. He went through the usual orientation, explaining a little of the routine and what my duties would be. The patients were middle-aged to elderly males with minor behavior problems. I was to be the first female employee to work on this ward. The past policy was that male employees worked on male wards and females worked only with female patients.

Mr. Coe cautioned me about several of the patients, whose behavior was occasionally unpredictable. He had once been a prizefighter, with his own set of unpredictable traits, having previously worked at Camarillo State Hospital, but transferred to Modesto when it opened in 1947. At first he was uncertain how to deal with a woman on his ward. I could tell by his orientation that he had been advised about my *mistaken notion* of patient abuse. He didn't mention it, nor did I, but he was on guard. We settled into a silent truce, and I was determined to win his trust. Soon, due to a mix-up on my part, he became convinced that he had probably gotten the flake of the trainee class.

One of my major duties was to help the patients with their personal care, bathing, grooming and dressing. Some of them were incontinent so I set up a retraining schedule. The second morning, I tackled oral hygiene. Only a few seemed to have their own personal toothbrush. It took an hour to get the new brushes individual's name and then have those able brush their teeth. It was obvious that no attention had been paid to oral hygiene in a long time, possibly years. When I tried to help the five or six patients, who wore dentures, I nearly lost my breakfast. As distasteful as it was, gagging and swallowing hard, I was determined to do my job.

I donned a pair of rubber gloves and got a gallon bucket of warm soapy water. Gritting my teeth, I removed everyone's dentures and placed them in the bucket to soak, changing the water several times. By using a long handled brush I was able to scrub the dentures without undue handling. I could tell it was going to take several soakings to get them really clean. Some were so crusted they needed extra attention. I brushed and scrubbed and rinsed.

Finally satisfied that they were as clean as I could get them, I lined them all up on the narrow shelf in the bathroom. They looked pretty good, considering. I was proud of the improvement, thinking how much better they would feel to the owners. I could swear they all looked like they were smiling at me while sitting all in a row.

Mr. Coe came down to the bathroom to see what was taking me so long. We stood side by side looking at five or six sets of teeth smiling back at us. I heard him suck in his breath and give a big sigh. Trying to identify which set of teeth belonged to which patient was all together impossible. I'll not tell you what Mr. Coe, or the dentist who was brought in to help identify the dentures, had to say about female trainees. I began to wonder if I really was cut out for this line of work. Regardless of the initial mix-up, I continued to see that every one brushed their teeth and or dentures daily, one set at a time.

Lovers

1927-1965

Any story or recounting of my life and times would be remiss if I didn't dedicate some pages remembering my wonderful friends and lovers. Of course, I have to be careful here…not to leave anyone out who might feel slighted. My dear friend Marianne, who has listened to me faithfully over tea and tears for the past two years, suggested that I write an entire book on the above subject. Perhaps I will do just that.

At an early age I had crushes on neighbor boys, teachers, movie stars, older brothers or fathers of friends, and fantasy characters. I only demanded that they be completely unreachable. It was so safe to yearn for Vaughan Monroe as he sang *Racing with the* For an entire year I was hopelessly in love with Danny Kaye after seeing him in the movie, *Up in Arms*, with Dinah Shore. I, along with millions of other bobby soxers, swooned as Frankie crooned, *I'll never smile again.* I faced a real dilemma when I first saw James Dean in *Rebel without a Cause* and Marlon Brando in *On the Waterfront* the same week in 1954. I guess that was my "bad boy" phase. I had two crushes that are still with me today—Paul Newman, and of course, the Heartbreak Hotel King himself, Elvis Presley. Never mind that Elvis is gone; he lives on in my memories and on countless CDs. Thank goodness I never had to make a choice, I'm hooked on them both.

I never had a problem recognizing that a crush was just that, and the good part was that there was no risk involved. No one expected me to show up at the Friday night movie with Elvis as my date. Crushes are for filling up the empty spaces and are available whenever there is a void. Since I had control over the drama of a crush, I used them to soothe my soul and help get over the bumps in the road of romance. When a real romance went sour and/or failed to materialize, I could listen to Frankie sing just to me and feel loved once again. It was right, when Paul Newman married Joanne, since we were never destined to meet in person and he deserved happiness. Things might have been different had we met first.

This is not a sexy, tell-all, sort of book, so I'll be gentle. I will share some firsts, but don't expect too much. I was about eleven years old when I got my first kiss and it came from Erwin Smith. He had been living in a state home in Seattle for some time when my Aunt Katy and Uncle Lon brought him home one spring day to live with them. Over the years they had dozen of children at one time or the other staying with them. Erwin was a tall, nice looking, but very immature, sixteen year-old, with a troubled past.

We had gone swimming at the beach near Langley dock. The kiss was unexpected and very gentle, but it frightened me. He just turned my face towards him and gave me a smack on the lips. Nothing was said and later I wondered if it really happened. Even then I knew that he had to be a little weird to kiss an eleven year old! He gave me a nice bracelet for Christmas, but I really wanted a bicycle like the one he had. I don't know what happened at my aunt's, but by the next spring he was suddenly gone. My mother told me he was sent back to the home and my uncle gave his bicycle to my brother, Floyd.

The summer I was fifteen, Frankie Del Pozzi became my first real boyfriend. His family was from Seattle and his father had bought beachfront at Mutiny Bay and planned to build a resort. We spent every free moment together swimming and bicycling between our two homes. Returning from a short visit to Seattle, he gave me a ring. It actually was a man's ring with a little chipped diamond setting. I didn't think the ring was very pretty, but it was the first I had ever gotten as a gift. The diamond fell out about a week later, so he brought me another ring just like the first one. During the hot summer months we got kissing down to a fine art. The romance was over when he had to return to the city at the start of the school year.

119

One romance that I still remember with fond memories took place the spring and summer of 1944. Donny Snyder and I were steadies. We both were employed at Cook's Creamery, I, as a waitress and Donny worked in the back processing milk products. He was shy, a big tease and loved western and hillbilly music. He built a small radio station, highly illegal, and broadcasted his music whenever he liked. During work one morning a customer told me to turn the radio to station 540AM. There we heard *The Voice of Prairie Center* with Donny Snyder, dedicating the broadcast to Mary Chase. As flattered, as I should have been, I was totally embarrassed as only a teenager can be.

I stayed in town with my girl friend, Gladys during the time I worked at the Creamery since my family lived in the country. Donny started walking me home after work. At first we just held hands and after a month or so we moved to the kissing phase. One evening a co-worker and I talked him in to using the Creamery's van to take us to a dance about 20 miles away. The owners heard about our outing and the next day fired all three of us. Don was a valuable employee and they rehired him in a day or so. It was a week before they asked me to come back. For some unknown reason they assumed that I was the instigator. When school started in the fall Donny and I broke up, but we remained friends. He went into the service and I eventually heard he had married.

Being a virgin was serious business in the 1940's. To borrow an observation made by Edith Bunker, from the TV hit *All in the Family,* "There were those that did, and those that did not." I often wondered if those that did were having more fun then those who did not. However, without really discussing it with anyone, I was determined to be one of those who did not. Staunchly, all through high school and beyond, I defended my virtue. Even Fort Knox could not have been guarded more diligently. I tried to figure out how one would know which girls did and which did not. There were a few who were considered easy, no problem there, but what about my friends and classmates? I think this may have been the beginning of the "Don't ask! Don't tell!" custom.

One afternoon my friend Neva and I were discussing life in general and sex in particular. "Don't you get tired of all the boys trying to get fresh with you?" I asked while we rehashed our dates of the night before. "Don't you wonder what David Whitehead would do if you let him?"

"Oh, David never tries anything," said Neva, "and besides, I'm not that kind of girl." Over the next couple years I heard her say that many times.

A few years ago, at the age of 70+ a group of us were talking about the good old days and our youth. I made a remark to Neva about what a sexy fox she had been. "Hey, I wasn't that kind of girl!" Some beliefs die hard, and it was still important to this twice married, grandmother of four, for us to know that she didn't sleep around when she was a teenager.

In my senior year of high school, Joe Rossi was my constant companion. He was stationed at Oak Harbor Naval Air Base as a parachute rigger. Our time together was spent playing cards with my parents, or sitting in his car necking. I was attracted to him for his dark good looks and his Brooklyn accent. I believe he was under the impression that we would eventually marry. However, I was not the least interested in marrying at that time, and to prove that I wasn't ready, my major complaint about Joe was that he was too short and that he didn't dance. While I was in my teens I had the idea that I would dance my way through life. My father seemed disappointed when Joe and I finally broke up and I started looking elsewhere for Mr. Right. My father didn't dance either.

In the spring of 1946 I met Teddy Webber, a young merchant marine sailor. His ship was briefly in port in Seattle. I was mad for him. He had one aim in life and that was to relieve me of the burden of my virginity. Ted might have succeeded, but he made a fatal mistake when he let me know he was engaged to his high school sweetheart in San Pedro, California. When his ship left for England I swore off sailors for good. Four months later I heard from one of his shipmates that Ted had drowned while swimming off the coast of Italy.

I was working for a lithograph company, taking a few college classes and sharing an apartment with two other girls. About six or seven of us formed a close group, living in the same apartment building. We were all around twenty-years of age and having a nonsensical time. After Ted left, I concentrated on my love affair (sic) with Danny Kaye, when a strange phenomena seemed to take over our group—like the animals boarding Noah's Ark—one by one became two by two.

Skippy married Doug, a sailor from New Zealand, just after Thanksgiving; then Neva and Bill had a Christmas wedding. The following month I went to Portland, Oregon to be bridesmaid for Jessie and Kenny. At the wedding, I met a good-looking truck driver, named Sandy, who pushed Danny Kaye out of the picture. Dottie and Joe surprised us when they announced that they would be next to tie the knot.

Weddings are contagious, so Sandy and I decided "what the hell?" and followed suit, although we barely knew one another. Obviously we married for all the wrong reasons. On our wedding night I found out that what I had been protecting so diligently for the past five years was no big deal to my new husband. I think we both realized after the first couple of months that we had done a dumb thing; however, by this time I was pregnant and I buckled down to my new role of expectant mother. Less than two years later our marriage was over and I had two beautiful baby girls, and no husband. Sandy proved to be as uninterested in being a father as he had been in being a husband, and dropped off the radar screen for the next twenty some years.

Being a single mother took up most of my time. I moved back to my parents' home on Whidbey Island and eventually moved into a small house of my own. The days were busy with my little girls and a part time job, but the evenings were lonely.

I soon met Woody, and a year later in January, 1951, we married and moved to Oregon, where he started a small logging company. Woody was a caring husband and a wonderful father to my two girls. Our daughter, Betty, was born the next fall in McMinnville, Oregon. The next summer we followed the lumber industry to northern California and our son Paul was born in Eureka in 1953. Woody got the contract to log the redwoods, near Crescent City, in preparation for a new highway, so we moved to Fort Dick. Although our little family seemed complete, I became pregnant with our fifth child the spring of 1954. I wrote several essays about Woody's fight with cancer and my struggles following his death. I believe had he lived, this would have been the end of my story about lovers.

So it was, I found myself alone again at 27 years of age, this time with five young children to take care of. I fell into a deep depression, but the children's needs kept me going. For the first two years after the death of my husband, I worked as waitress in a neighborhood bar. Many of the regular customers were loggers and few were single. The men at the bar were looking for a good time, not to suddenly become a father of many children. Unhappy as I was, I found that after a few highballs, the lights were a little brighter, the music louder, and the men were better looking.

The next five years were spent looking for Mr. Goodbar in all the wrong places. There was a parade of losers with a very short shelf life, most of them forgettable, and not significant to my life. For over a year I had a long distance romance with what I believed was my Prince Charming. We made elaborate plans to move to Venezuela and even set the wedding date, only to have him turn back into a frog, when I discovered he was already married and the father of two young sons. He taught me many things during our fatal courtship. The most important being, that if something sounds too good to be true, it probably is.

I had the illusion, during this bleak period, that a man, any man, would be better than going it alone. I learned a lot about the seedy side of life from these years. By the time I was 32, I was burned out by the bar scene and ready to settle down. I was so very lonely and tired of trying to make it on my own. I wanted someone to take care of me, both financially and emotionally.

It was then that a wonderful turn of events, that completely changed my life, came my way. No, it wasn't a man; it was a job, a job that turned into a career. My new career gave me hope, self-confidence and a promise of a better life. I developed a passion, something outside of myself, that completely changed my outlook. Suddenly I had no need or time to worry about being without a man. I was caught up in getting an education and advancing at work. At last, I liked me, just the way I was.

Two years later, when I wasn't looking, I met George at work. We married in 1965 and we merged our two families. The merger and our life together deserve its own essay.

The Merger

July 26, 1965

When I first saw the name Van Loon on the staffing board, which was posted weekly in front of the supervisor's office, I was a little intrigued. Having gone to school in Coupeville, Washington, I knew many classmates of Dutch decent, but had never come across a Van Loon before. I studied the name thinking, "That's almost a neat name." The Loon part threw me at first.

I was working as a Psychiatric Technician Trainee at Modesto State Hospital and the next week would be my last ward assignment before completing the yearlong training program. I saw that Mr. George Van Loon was listed as the person in charge of B-5. As most of us in the training program did when receiving a new assignment, I questioned some of my classmates, who had previously worked a rotation on B-5. My major concern was how the staff treated the patients and the trainees. I was told that the patients living on his ward were elderly with many physical problems and required a great deal of assistance. I was assured that they were treated well by the staff. I vaguely remember that when I was on one of my former wards, Don Coe had been my supervisor and I had heard a little about his ex-son-in-law who was assigned to B-5. I soon realized my new boss and his son-in-law were one and the same.

Someone pointed George out to me one morning as we were making our way to class. He was standing outside B-5 talking to a doctor who was making his rounds. I glanced down the corridor noting a tall technician; rail thin; one of my first thoughts was that he needed fattening up. He had dark hair with a high widow's peak, and brown eyes nearly obscured by horned rimed glasses, giving him a slight owlish appearance. Stretching my imagination, he reminded me of Clark Kent looking for a phone booth. George was dressed in white pants, long sleeved white shirt with a black tie, the standard uniform of the male technicians.

The next Monday I reported to my new assignment and received my orientation. Things went well and over the next couple months I learned a great deal about my boss. He was kind to the patients and had a reputation of not tolerating any mistreatment. I mentally gave him a gold star, and we were off to a good start. It was common knowledge that he had recently gone through a rough divorce, and had gained custody of his four young children, which was unusual in 1963. He also had a teenage stepson, Pat, who was a frequent visitor. Here was a man who was kind to old men and faced his responsibilities; and he was tall. However, one day I overheard him tell a friend that he'd had it with women, and he had no intention of becoming involved with anyone again until his kids were grown.

Thinking I should get my AA degree, I started taking classes at Modesto Junior College in September. A co-worker talked me into joining the State Hospital Bowling League. I was very busy with the children, school and now bowling one night a week. In the meantime, I was having a growing feelings for George and could tell he was interested, regardless of his comment about women.

A national tragedy finally triggered our mutual attraction. We were at work on Thursday morning in November, when we heard the tragic news that President Kennedy had been shot. In horror we watched the drama unfold on T.V. whenever we could spare a few minutes throughout the day. As our workday ended, we were reluctant to say goodbye and agreed to meet later that evening for a drink and to talk about the event. I felt close to George as we shared our feelings, and it was the first time I thought seriously about a possible relationship.

Our first official date was for New Year's Eve, 1963. We had been invited to a party at the home of a couple we knew. I had a new dress and took special care with my hair and make-up, as I was getting ready for my big date. George picked me up and I introduced him to my children. Chris was impressed with the horn-rimed glasses, telling me later that she thought he looked very professional. We had decided to go the party with my friend, Ruby and her husband, Bob. George drove us to their home. We had a quiet drink together and gossiped about people we knew in common. Bob planned to drive, so after checking the home address where the party was being held, we set out on our way.

While we had been at Ruby's home, patches of wet fog started settling in. The fog moved in fast and it wasn't long before we were lost in gray nothingness without shape or sound. Carefully Bob drove aimlessly about, unable to recognize the neighborhood or read the street addresses. Finally, deciding to give up, we unexpectedly reached our destination. Cars were leaving and the host came out and told us the party was breaking up due to the fog, as everyone was anxious to get home. The fizzled first date may have been a hint of things to come.

From then on we had a standing "date" on my bowling night. George and his parents shared a house, and his father was the primary sitter when he was at work. His mother was still employed. Although George wasn't interested in joining the team, he would come down to the alley after things had settled down at his home and his children were in bed. We would join other couples for after game activities. Not very exciting, however, with the many responsibilities each of us had; it was about all the time we could squeeze out of our busy schedules.

I invited George and his children over to watch T.V. one evening. When the doorbell rang and I answered it, there he stood with Timothy, one year old, in his arms, Michael, 8, in front, and Sharon and Karon, 11, one on each side of him, identical bookends. Cautiously, they eyed my five, Sharon Ann 16, Christine 15, Betty 13, Paul 11, and Janice 9. Betty knew Sharon from school, and it wasn't long before the others became acquainted. As George and I tried to visit, little Tim still unsteady on his chubby legs, spent his time crawling up and down the brick steps leading into the family room causing required safety measures to be put into place.

During the courtship, we mingled the children and our parents, trying to determine if a merger could possibly work. Although George's children seemed to approve of me, they were still hoping that their mother and dad would get back together. The twins' favorite movie was "The Parent Trap," staring Haley Mills. Haley, playing twin roles in the movie, manages to get their parents back together. Sadly life is not like a movie.

We all enjoyed camping, fishing and boating and quickly started a family tradition of vacations at the lake or river. If we were to marry, housing would certainly be a problem, but love is blind and fools rush in where angels fear to tread. A year and a half later, we were married.

Our Wedding

Our Kids at Our Wedding

We decided to enlarge the three-bedroom house I had recently purchased, by enclosing the large patio and making it into the fourth bedroom, soon to be known as the 'dorm'. First the 'Girls' Dorm,' then as Sharon Ann and Christine married and moved out, it became the 'Boys' Dorm.'

The first couple of years I worked the afternoon shift so one of us would be home at all times. To say that these were busy times is, of course, an understatement; hectic might be more descriptive. I had started the nursing program and seemed to meet myself coming and going. Christine made me a grandmother at 39 and was a frequent visitor. As a co-worker once observed as she came to pick up one of our girls to baby sit, our evening supper table looked like a full Thanksgiving Day meal. We had six teenagers in high school in 1969. Once, with the car full of kids, I stopped at a Service Station and was asked by the clerk if I was taking a group of kids on a church picnic.

Nine, strong willed individuals, living in 1,700 sq feet of space led to many problems. George and I set up some rules, that later backfired, and a schedule for keeping house. The household chores were divided among the four girls and were changed weekly. The assignments were #1 laundry/bathroom, #2 living room, #3 family room, and #4 the kitchen. The girl assigned to the kitchen helped me with dinner each night and saw to the dishes after. I used this time to talk about school and what was going on in their lives. The boys were assigned trash, wood for the fireplace and yard work. The laundry presented a problem with four girls all about the same size. Janice jokingly told me that in gym class she was surprised to discover that all bras didn't come with a nametag.

We were rather strict about bedtime, showers, curfew and mealtime. It was impossible to set rules that could apply to all, with the wide range of ages. One day coming home from work, I found Betty, then 17, sitting on the porch steps looking dejected. "What's the problem, Bets?

"I'm so mad," she started, "I'd run away from home, except I'm not allowed out of the court."

Years later, for our 18th wedding anniversary all ten children threw us a surprise party and we were roasted and teased about all our rules. Looking back, I realize that some of the restrictions were more in keeping with inmates in an institution. In our defense, it was a changing world, and in the late 60's the Vietnam War, the Beatles and the hippie movement had strong influence over young people. One of our ongoing battles was over the length of Paul and Mike's hair. Even more serious was getting everyone in and out of the one shower before nine o'clock deadline. I laugh now at how I worried about the girls going to bed with wet heads.

There was the ordinary bickering and teenage complaints, some jealousies. It was almost impossible to give each child the individual attention he should have had. On the other hand, the children grew close and filled some of the void. Individual trips to the dentist or shopping were quality time and Karon gloated over the phrase "only child." She first used it after riding to the hospital to have her broken leg set, and sat in the front seat between her dad and me.

Money was tight, and we economized as much as possible. I mixed powdered with regular milk and stored it in the milk carton, fooling no one. There were lots of casseroles to stretch the main course. There were no picky eaters. At mealtime everyone sat down together, and were expected to excuse him or herself before leaving the table. With growing appetites they would make their way around the kitchen, fixing after school snacks, looking much like a swarm of locust descending on a field of corn.

We loved camping and I soon grew tired of sleeping in a tent so one of our first luxuries was a little travel trailer. It was still necessary to put up three tents, one for boys, one for girls and one to change and store extra equipment. The next year we got a ski boat and the boys rescued a small rowboat from the river. Getting ready for a long weekend to the lake was an experience. We had the traditional station wagon pulling the ski boat fully loaded. George had a 62' Chevy pick-up loaded with the tents, cold boxes and an assortment of other equipment, while still pulling the trailer. As we caravanned down the highway it looked as if we were going on a safari.

Holidays were important and difficult to manage, sharing time with George's ex-wife and mother of his children. The first year we established that Thanksgiving was our big family get-together. Our parents, and George's Aunt and Uncle, rounded out the guest list. Over the years that tradition has endured, and no matter where family members now live they try to make it home for turkey and reconnecting. Our parents, aunts and uncles are all gone, but we now have four generations filling our home with laughter and love.

We lived in our first house at 2041 Wally Court in Modesto for five years. When Modesto State Hospital closed, we relocated to Porterville, California, where we went to work at Porterville Developmental Center. It was a difficult transition, going from working with the mentally ill to working with the mentally retarded.

The older children were beginning to find their own way—to college, marriage or into the service. I was in the final year of nursing school when suddenly we were down to only three children left at home. One day, driving home from work, I had a near panic attack brought on from the empty nest syndrome. By 1976, our youngest Tim, was the only child living at home. I was back in school completing my B.S. in Hospital Administration. George was Supervisor of the Workshop, and I was working as Charge Nurse on the Pediatric Unit.

In this short essay I have not written about the individual and unique personalities of each child. I'll save that for another time. Those years, when the house was over flowing, and there was never enough time or money, went by so quickly; they were the best of times and the most difficult. It hardly seems possible that over forty years have passed. Don't ask me if I would do it again if I had a choice, knowing what I know now. I'm not so sure, but I wouldn't have missed it for the world the first time around.

Thinking about those hectic days, I remember one morning I sat down for a quiet cup of coffee, after everyone else left for school. Tim was playing quietly with his trucks in the family room. I happened to glance up towards the ceiling. There were several long strands of spaghetti dangling from the overhead chandelier. I remember how surprised I was. How in the world? Sighing, I decided I didn't want--or need to know. I'd just enjoy the peace and quiet while I could and gather strength for what ever came next.

Lunch at Carmen's!

June 1969

Bonnie thought of it first, then, Barbara joined in. "We've worked hard all year and now it is time to celebrate," was the theme of their campaign to have a group lunch the last day of class. The nursing class of 1969 had just completed the second-semester at Modesto Junior College and would be leaving for the summer break. There is something about sharing a year of hard work, the ups and downs, the disappointment, and achievement that bring together a group who normally have little in common.

The two-year Associate of Science Degree nursing program was a relatively new concept, and had met with major objections from the State Licensing Board of Examiners. Graduates of the four-year Bachelor of Science and the traditional three-year Diploma School of Nursing fought the inception of the new classification. Times were changing however, and diploma schools were on the way out; young women were no longer willing to give up any resemblance of a normal life for three years. As attractive and desirous as the four-year degree program was, many could not afford the cost. Stay-at-home moms were looking to get back into the job market, and there was an army of untapped resources waiting for an opportunity.

There was a critical need for nurses in all aspects of the medical world. The A.S. program was designed to attract mature return to school students, as well as fresh high school graduates on the fast track to a career. The program was no pushover. It demanded a full year of pre-requisites followed by four semesters of nursing theory and clinical experience. Graduates are required to take the same state board's examination as the diploma, and four year candidates do before being licensed. The class of 1969 was the third that M.J.C. had offered, and I was smack dab in the middle of it.

I still worked at Modesto State Hospital as a Psychiatric Technician. If you read my earlier essay about how I came to find my vocation, you may recall that I considered it almost a miracle that led me to my present job. I was absolutely dedicated to working with psychotic and institutionalized individuals. I had moved from PT Trainee to LPT and in 1965 promoted to PT1, a shift lead position. MSH needed Registered Nurses and offered a wonderful opportunity for employees, once they were accepted in the nursing program. You were required to work half time, but receive full salary while attending class for a two-year period. It was available for those wishing to become teachers, social workers or physiologists as well.

On the home front there were still seven of our ten children in school. Everyone pitched in and though it was an unbelievable hectic time we managed somehow. I did most of my studying in the early hours of the morning, sometimes hiding out in our camping trailer whenever I had a big test coming up. So here we were, the first year was over, grades were in and I was looking at only two additional classes over the summer. A party sounded good to me.

Barbara, the organizer, caught me as I was heading for my car. "Will you have time to book the restaurant for the entire class before Friday? And," she added, "maybe arrange to be there to welcome everyone."

I thought a moment. "I don't have a class Friday morning; I can get there a little early." We had polled the class and had agreed on the location. I was pleased to be asked to take care of this simple task and looked forward to a good time the following Friday.

Carmen's Mexican Restaurant in McHenry Village was one of my favorite places, and my husband and I often had dinner there on special occasions. On Wednesday I called and made reservations for Friday at 11:45 am for 24 students and two of the instructors.

"Did you remember to make reservations?" wondered Bonnie as we dashed to the parking lot following Physiology Lab late Thursday afternoon.

"Everything is set; I took care of it last night." I assured her. "See you tomorrow."

Friday dawned bright and warm. I took special care with my hair as I dressed for lunch. I left home a few minutes early to check on everything and to act as unofficial hostess. Arriving at Carmen's I found the long table set for 26 in the center of the main dining room. Water glasses were filled and bowls of salsa and chips were placed around the table. It all looked very inviting. I sat down to wait for the crowd.

Minutes past; I glanced at my watch. It was nearly 12:00 o'clock and no one had arrived. I wondered what could be keeping everyone. The waitress checked to see what the delay was. I assure her the others were on the way. I couldn't resist any longer and took one of the chips and dipped it deep into the nearest bowl of salsa. With the loaded chip on its way to my mouth a horrible realization struck me!

We had agreed on Minnie's, not Carmen's. The salsa slid off the chip and plopped on the white tablecloth; I stuffed the chip into my mouth and bolted for the door. I found a public telephone booth around the corner and called Minnie's asking to speak to Barbara. Her voice sounded a little snippy when she finally came on the line. "I thought you had reservations for us. They had to set up after we all got here."

I tried to explain, "I made reservations at Carmen's."

"Well you can eat there if you wish," she paused, "but we are staying here at Minnie's. I have to get back to the table; the waitress is starting to take our orders."

Not much help there," I thought to myself as I hung up the phone and looked back at the restaurant. I thought about leaving town, there was no way I could go back into Carmen's and face the waitress, 26 empty chairs and the salsa drip on the tablecloth. I called the restaurant and I could see the hostess answering the phone. I ducked my head and told her that the lunch had been cancelled. With a vague reference to a sudden "mix-up," and a hurried apology, I got off the phone as quickly as I could. I stood in the hot phone booth wondering how this could have happened and decided to skip lunch. There was no rational way I could explain why I was waiting at Carmen's while everyone else was at Minnie's.

A few weeks later it was our 4th wedding anniversary and George assumed we would have dinner at Carmen's. As usual, he asked me to make reservations for our big night. I had been too embarrassed and had never told him about the luncheon fiasco. He was a little puzzled, but seemed pleasantly surprised when I offered to cook his favorite dinner at home.

Porterville, California

1970 - 1991

PORTERVILLE STATE HOSPITAL
Porterville, California

INTER-OFFICE MEMO
October 30, 1979

TO: All Who Receive Administrative Manual Issuances

FROM: James T. Shelton, M.D., Executive Director

SUBJECT: Coordinator of Nursing Services

Our Coordinator of Nursing Services, Pauline Longsworth, R.N., left us on September 28, 1979. Mrs. Frances Carter, R.N. has been acting in that position since that time. On Friday, October 26, 1979 a selection panel consisting of Mrs. Taylor - Clinical Director, Mr. Mr. Eckert - Personnel Officer, Mr. Flores - Affirmative Action Coordinator, and I, interviewed 5 candidates for the position of Coordinator of Nursing Services. Our selection was Mrs. Mary Van Loon who currently is in the position of Health Services Supervisor in Program I. Effective November 1, 1979 she will become our new Coordinator of Nursing Services.

Mrs. Van Loon, besides having her Registered Nurse diploma, possesses a Bachelor of Science Degree from Chapman College and is currently registered in a Master of Arts program at the University of Redlands. She began her career in the field of nursing as a Psychiatric Technician Trainee in April of 1962, becoming a Psychiatric Technician and promoting to Senior Psychiatric Technician at the Modesto State Hospital in March of 1967. She remained there until that facility closed.

Mrs. Van Loon took a short break from the nursing field and then joined the Porterville State Hospital in December of 1970 as a Psychiatric Technician II. She obtained her Registered Nurse diploma through attendance at the College of Sequoias nursing program and promoted to Registered Nurse III in December of 1977. She has acted as Unit Manager of Ward B in the Acute Hospital, served as Acting Nursing Coordinator in Program I between December of 1978 and March of 1979, and is currently Health Services Specialist in Program I.

She was selected as a member of the Department of Developmental Service task force in setting up the Health Service Specialist and Coordinator of Nursing Services positions. She is also active as Training Coordinator in Program I and has had experience as a QMRP. Mrs. Van Loon has worked closely with the Coordinator of Licensure in Program I for the JCAH and licensing surveys. She has developed new nursing procedures to upgrade care and assure compliance of these demands in our acute hospital. She has also completed a number of management workshops and training courses since being at Porterville State Hospital.

Mrs. Van Loon will report in line to the Executive Director and be functionally supervised by Mrs. Rowena Taylor, Clinical Director. Her name will be reflected in the next revision of HB 14-R and in committee assignments in HB 18-R.

JTS:ot

Porterville State Hospital - Memo of Promotion, October 1979

STATE OF CALIFORNIA—HEALTH AND WELFARE AGENCY

George Deukmejian, Governor

DEPARTMENT OF DEVELOPMENTAL SERVICES
PORTERVILLE STATE HOSPITAL
P.O. BOX 2000, PORTERVILLE, CA 93258
(209) 784-2000
TTY (209) 784-2000

April 19, 1983

RN-LVN Professional Staff Organization
Mary Van Loon, Coordinator of Nursing Services
P. O. Box 2000
Porterville, CA 93258

Dear Mrs. Van Loon,

Please extend our thanks to all the members of your organization for their
efforts in landscaping the 100' section of the Blue Heron Parkway which was
accomplished over the past weekend. Perhaps your example will inspire other
PSH organizations to undertake the project for their own groups.

We believe the parkway will be an outstanding attraction in Southeastern
Tulare County and a source of pride for all of us at PSH when it is completed
late this year.

The time, money and physical efforts donated by the RN-LVN Professional Staff
are greatly appreciated.

Sincerely,

James T. Shelton, M.D.
Executive Director

JTS:cg
cc: Mr. Jones

Porterville State Hospital Letter, 1983

And Now--The Rest of the Story

April 1983

Friday morning dawned bright and sunny, unseasonably warm for the middle of April, and the temperature rose steadily throughout the day. By three p.m. the gentle breeze of the morning had disappeared and the sun beat down on our small group gathered at the roadside. It was a pitifully small turnout--eight tired female nurses and one 90 year-old volunteer. Today was the day the RN Professional Staff had elected to do their share of beautifying the new Blue Heron Parkway and I was in charge.

Our designated 100 foot long by 18 foot deep section had been plowed and stood ready for the "master gardeners." The RN Organization had put together a cookbook to raise the money for the purchase of the plants and trees. It never made the bestseller list and out of desperation the nurses bought most of the books themselves; twenty-four years later I still have several copies. The coordinator of the project, Mr. Jones, had given us the general plan and we were locked into a common design with specific plants.

This day Mr. Jones was nowhere to be found and we were on our own. The deep holes for the trees were ready and it took two or three of us to drag each of the five-gallon containers with the young poplar trees over to the holes. It was no easy task to loosen the soil, pull the ball out of the container and stand the new tree upright. But with persistence and determination soon all seven were in place. While Linda and Doris shoveled dirt around the bare roots, Phyllis and Jeannie were digging holes for the white oleander plants. There were flats of African Daisies and gallon cans with small shrubs all waiting to be planted. It seemed like a great deal of work for the few of us who had shown up.

It wasn't long before we had all worked up a sweat, but things were coming along. I put Irene in charge of the fertilizer, with me in charge of the watering. As the holes were dug, Irene shoveled in the fertilizer and I would drag the large hose over and run in a gallon or two of water. As the water quickly dispersed, the shrub or plant was dropped in. The surgical nurses were used to working as a team and they soon had most of the shrubs planted and waiting to have the soil packed around the roots. The hose that I dragged around was attached to a water pipe that stood upright next to the fence. The water pipe was for irrigating purposes and the mouth of the faucet was about 4 inches across. I had plenty of pressure and filled each hole quickly.

Hot and sweaty as the work was, we were determined to complete the planting that evening. I was beginning to worry about our ninety-year-old volunteer who had commanded the wheelbarrow and brought in additional soil.

The Hospital Clinical Director, Ro Taylor R.N., supported the Professional Group and had said that she might stop by on her way home from work. She was my supervisor and my mentor; I owed her a good deal. "Did Ro say for sure she would stop?" Sharon asked for the third time.

"Not only did she say she planned to stop by, but she said she was bringing her gardening shoes and would stay and help."

"Well, she better get here soon, we need all the help we can get; I've about had it."

"Is that her coming?" wondered Jeanne, "I never saw that car before." It was indeed Ro in her brand new Renault sedan--the car so new it didn't have license plates. The car was bright red, small, compact, and close to the ground, like its owner. Ro was a just five feet tall with bright red hair and a contagious laugh.

She pulled up and parked close to where we were working. The front window on the driver's side was rolled down. Ro's arrival cheered the work group as she quickly grabbed a hoe and started breaking up clods of dirt. By this time most of the plants were in and they all needed additional water. I was kept busy dragging the heavy hose from one shrub to the next.

I could see that I might be here far into night. I'm one of those people who figures that if two of something is good, four will be better.

I laid the nozzle close to a newly planted tree. *I think I'll turn the water pressure up and get this over with*, I thought to myself, giving the handle a couple quick turns. I could hear the water pouring into the ground. It was then I saw our volunteer stagger under the weight of a full wheelbarrow and moved over to assist him, proud of my multi-tasking.

Everyone was moving about and the end was in sight. I don't remember who saw it first and called out a warning. I turned. The pressure had blown the hose loose and the strong spout of water arched gracefully straight through the open window of Ro's car. I ran forward and turned the water off. Jeanne rushed over to the car and opened the front door to get a better look. As she opened the door the water came pouring out like water over a dam. The car was one of those that you step down into and it was completely full. Several of us grabbed empty cans and started bailing. When we had bailed out all we could, Jeanne got some beach towels that she had in the trunk of her car and we used them to soak up the remainder. I probably apologized half a dozen times.

"Did you see how the water shot straight into the car?" marveled Linda, "You couldn't have had better aim if you had tried."

The brand new floor mats were pulled up, shaken and wrung out, which didn't seem to help. We were full of advice, but Ro was so calm; I thought she was in shock. "I'm going to take my car home and Bill can take out the floor mats and dry out the inside of the car."

"Ro," I could barely meet her eyes. "I am so sorry; I don't know how this could happen."

"Stop, Mary! It's only a car. No one was hurt," Ro said as she climbed into her damp vehicle and turned on the motor. Thank goodness it still worked. She pulled away from the parkway and headed down the highway. We stood in silence watching the little car disappear with water spewing out from all sides.

Jack Frost and Other Real Life Heroes

January 1972

The new painting caught my eye as I entered the room. The colors were vivid. I moved loser, and carefully studied the scene. Stick figures, Grandma Moses style, it must have been painted by a budding genius. I could barely make out the signature at the bottom of the picture, Lee. I smiled, one of my very favorite artists. Just then the door opened and Lee came in, handsome, with blond hair and beautiful brown eyes. "Hi, Grandma," the future Picasso greeted me with a hug.

Good Grandma said, "Did you paint this picture, Lee?" careful not to label it, as I was not quite sure what I was looking at.

"It's Jack Frost," he explained carefully, as if to a very dumb child, "you know, he comes at night and puts snow and frost on everything. He's from the North Pole."

I was a little rusty at this grandma thing, so I plunged on, "That's a nice story, Lee," said Bad Grandma.

"It's not a story! There really is a Jack Frost!" His little face got a very anxious look. I missed the signs of *Oh! Oh! Better not go there*, so I repeated, "That's a wonderful story, Lee."

His face became twisted, with tears not far behind. "Jack Frost really does come at night, Mrs. Peterson says so!" Mrs. Peterson was Lee's teacher, and the final authority on nearly everything, since Lee had started the first grade.

I attempted to explain what I really meant, but Lee would have none of that. I reached out to stop him, as he grabbed the picture off the refrigerator, tore it in two, and threw it in the trashcan. I was overcome with remorse, but the damage was done. His small shoulders were high as he stalked to his room and we could her him banging things around.

It didn't help much when my son-in-law told me that Lee has been questioning several childhood fantasies lately. I think my daughter was secretly pleased when Lee refused to kiss me goodnight, and I was sure she thought I needed to be punished.

Later, my daughter and son-in-law had a family meeting and decided to forgive me. I could stay the night.

Lee-Lee, April 1969

Several months later, the grand boys (three of them at that time) were spending a weekend with my husband and me. Weekend visits are educational for grandparents and a break for mom and dad. When grandkids go home you remember why, in the sudden stillness, it is not so bad being old.

The boys and I were on our way to the grocery store. They were in the back seat of our old station wagon, and I wasn't paying much attention to their chatter. Voices got a little loud, and I heard, "Is too!" "Is not!" Finally Scott, the youngest, nearly in tears said, "I'm going to ask Grandma!"

Lee, the artist takes over. "Grandma," he begins, "do you believe in Santa Claus?" Smart Grandma kicked in, "What do you think, Lee?"

"Where do Easter Bunnies get Easter Eggs?" The boy is on a roll! One by one he attacks each of his childhood heroes. I realize we are in serious meltdown. "My mom and dad buy my Christmas presents. I saw them in my mom's closet. They just pretend they are from Santa Claus. My mom bought our Easter Baskets."

By this time Scott, whimpering, had climbed over the seat, and was trying to get in my lap.

"There is no Tooth Fairy; my dad puts the dime under my pillow." I'm in major shock! This boy has been doing some hard thinking. "You know what, Grandma? I don't believe in any of that stuff. I only believe in two things. Do you want to know what they are?"

Careful here, I tell myself feeling like I was walking through a minefield. Holding my breath, "No, what two things do you believe in, Lee?"

"I believe in God…and Jack Frost!"

Talking Dirty

February 1974

Tom, four and a half, and Scott, who had just turned four, were playing with their cars on the floor behind the sofa where I sat reading. Suddenly there was some giggling. I tuned in on their conversation.

"Say something bad, Scott." Tommy starts. "Pee, Pee," both giggled. Then with a devilish grin, Scott dares Tom, "Now you."

Looking at me out of the corner of his eye, Tom whispers, "Poo poo." More laughs. I wonder where they can go from here.

"Say something else, Tom," Scott pleads. Quietly, I wait, finally Tom chocks out, "Underwear!" Gales of laughter follow, mostly mine.

Tom and Scott

Chopped Liver

Summer 1979

Tommy and Scott were staying with us for a week during summer vacation. I was really getting into this grandma thing. We dug worms, and went fishing at Balch Park up the mountain. I showed them how to capture rattlesnakes, and the day before, we had spent most of the afternoon on our houseboat at Lake Success. The boys had been swimming and playing in our pool and now were ready for a snack. I baked some cookies while they sat at the breakfast bar watching and waiting. Ice cold milk and warm cookies, what could be better?

Reaching for his fifth chocolate chip cookie Tom challenges Scott, "You think these are good, you should taste my Grandma McDonald's cookies." Scott, never to be out done, replies, "You ought to taste my Grandma Smith's brownies."

Back and forth, trying to outdo the other with praise for their separate grandma's cooking skills, while Grandma Van Loon, spatula in hand, wonders where she went wrong.

Home Sweet....

1978

I have always considered Whidbey Island as my "home", even though I was born and lived my first eight years in Livingston, California. "Home" means that place where a piece of myself has stayed and no matter where or what my life is I get a slight yearning whenever I hear or think about the island. I spent over twenty years there and my emotional ties continue to run deep. I kept the sweet memories tucked away as insurance that no matter how bad things got in the real world there was always a "perfect place" I could revisit in my daydreams. Rain on the rooftop, the lonesome sound of a distant foghorn or the smell of the ocean, all would immediately carry me back in time. My memory of the island was my anchor, that is, until one visit back after a twenty-three-year absence.

I had wanted to have my husband go with me so I could share my growing up years with him. He has his "Castle Street' and I have my "Whidbey Island" but due to personal reasons he couldn't make the trip, so my daughters Betty and Christine decided to tag along. It was a fun auto trip along the Oregon Coast and on into Washington State. We took our time and enjoyed the fantastic scenery and each other. The trip was full of laughs and mounting anticipation at returning to my hometown. Betty had the movie camera going. She missed my hot curlers tumbling off the roof of the car on I-5 and me scrambling to pick them up before they were run over, but not much else.

As we drove off the ferry at Clinton I felt my heart racing; I had a lump in my throat. Imagine my surprise and delight at spying a large "Welcome back, Chase" sign gracing the marquee of Cozy Corners Bar and Grille. I was totally overwhelmed at the thoughtfulness of my brother-in-law who must have arranged for the sign. That he used my maiden name was no surprise, to him and many others I would always be Mary Chase. I posed beneath the sign feeling a bit foolish, but a bit like a celebrity retuning to her hometown in triumph.

It was bittersweet to revisit scenes and sights from the past and especially sharing them with my daughters. I couldn't stop smiling as I relived so many fond memories. The girls delighted in my stories, which encouraged me to share even more.

It was the second day of exploring that we drove out to Freeland and came to where my family had lived for fifteen years. Pop had acquired the property in 1940 and had dreams of developing a tourist resort on the lakefront. Somehow he persuaded Mom that this was our destiny. The Chases now owned 100 acres of huckleberry brush, hundreds of stump, third growth fir, cedar and alder trees and millions of mosquitoes. The small lake was fed from an underground spring and was teaming with fresh water perch.

The dream of a resort would change many times over the years. Pop was the idea man, Mom was the straw boss and my brothers and I were the worker bees. I remember many of the schemes Pop came up with over the next 10 years, i.e. brooder chicks, laying hens, peat moss, a sawmill for shakes, mink and beaver pelts, trout, and/or a dairy farm. In 1955, as his volunteer work crew disappeared and reality set in, he sold his dream to a mainline "Wilderness Club" for a hunting retreat.

Although I had looked forward to this visit, I was ambivalent about seeing what changes had been made on the property. We parked at the side of the road and walked back to where the driveway had lead up to our house so many years ago. There was a "NO TRESSPASSING" sign hanging on a chain stretched across the narrow overgrown tire tracks. Saplings and undergrowth obscured the view. Obviously the road was seldom if ever used in the last ten years. So we decided to ignore the sign and quickly climbed over the chain.

As we slowly climb the gentle grade I was filled with emotions and felt my father's dream come alive. I listened, expecting to hear my mother calling me or to be challenged by my brother Bill to see who could reach the top of the hill first. When we reached the area where I thought our house had once stood only silence and the forest greeted us.

"Where's the house?" Betty asked, looking around.

"It was right over there." My throat tightened as I glanced around trying to get everything in perspective.

Christine pointed to a partially collapsed building off to the left. "Is that part of your house?" I could see it was what was left of our garage. The sides had rotted or been knocked down until the roof rested about four feet above the ground. I saw the remains of a small fire-pit and it was obvious that someone had crawled under the roof and sought shelter there. By the condition of the surrounding ground it had been used many times. I remembered how Pop and Floyd had built the garage first, before any of the other buildings, to store the equipment that we used to clear the land. It had never been completely finished, but stood without a door or glass in the window for nearly forty years.

The house was gone! I made my way slowly to where it actually had once stood. Nothing. Whether it had been moved or fell into ruins, I had no idea. I tried to picture the barn and the chicken houses and wondered what had become of them. All that work! All those long hours, weeks and years of struggle; falling trees and dragging brush, plowing the fields, carrying buckets of water from the lake until we hand dug the well, using kerosene lanterns while my mother settled a two year fight with the Defense Department to get permission to bring the electricity less than a thousand feet from the highway to our house—all in vain. Nature had reclaimed the land. There was nothing left, no evidence that my family had ever been here except for the tumbled down roof of the garage. Hot tears dropped silently from my eyes.

Betty stepped close to me. "What do you think happened to your house?"

A gentle wind rustled through treetops and pushed fallen leaves across the dry grass. Although the day was warm I hugged myself to stop shivering. I felt the forest mock me as it closed around us. I searched for an answer to Betty's question while wishing I had never come back.

Later that evening I thanked my brother-in-law for putting up the welcome sign on Cozy Corner's marquee and mentioned that I had my picture taken under it. "I want my husband to see it."

John looked at me like he didn't know what I was talking about. "What...? Oh that's so funny! You thought that was about you?" I didn't like his laugh. "Hey Ellen,' he called to his wife, "you gotta hear this. Mary thought the sign welcoming the rock group *'Chase'* was for her."

Riverbank, California

1991 - Present

One of Life's Little Oops

June 2003

As Volunteer Manager of Field Operations for AARP, I logged thousand of miles traveling throughout the United States. California has two corporate offices, one in Sacramento and the other in Pasadena, with satellite regional offices in San Diego, San Francisco and Santa Barbara. Weekly flights were the norm. I often flew SouthWest Airlines out of Sacramento, but almost as often would fly out of Oakland. My choice of which airport I used depended on the time of day of my scheduled flight since the distances were about the same. Commute traffic to and from the Bay area was a killer, adding as much as an hour either way to the normal hour and half trip.

This particular time I was in San Diego for a two or three day conference. The meeting finished sooner than expected. My flight home was booked for 5:05 P.M. As I approached the gate, I noticed that they had a 4 P.M. to Oakland just boarding. For a few dollars I was able to change my ticket. Settling in my seat, I smiled, pleased with myself for getting an earlier flight. As the plane was taking off my mind left the happenings of the day and jumped ahead. I knew my husband would be pleasantly surprised when I got home an hour before expected. That got me to thinking about the drive home and then I tried to visualize where I'd parked my car at the airport.

"No," I thought, "it wasn't economy parking; I must have used Park and Fly." Then realization hit. "Oh my God, I'm not parked at Oakland; I flew out of Sacramento!"

I tried to explain to the flight attendant that I needed to get off, that there had been a terrible mistake.

"Yes," I agreed, "I realized that I have a ticket for Oakland, but I really need to go to Sacramento. I don't want to go to Oakland! I made a mistake." I was quite adamant and several fellow passengers began looking at me with interest. Commute flights are normally pretty boring—take off, instructions on how to use your seat for a float in case the plane crash in the ocean, a bag of peanuts and a plastic cup of watered down Sprite. Not much variation. Since the flight attendant wasn't much help, I demanded to talk to the pilot. I believe in going to the top when you want something important done.

"The pilot is busy right now flying this aircraft, perhaps when we get airborne…" People were really looking my way, and I might have heard one man mutter something about old ladies traveling alone.

Did you know SouthWest Airlines has a policy against turning the plane around once it leaves the runway? I never knew that before, but it was fully explained to me. The whole scene put me in mind of my Aunt Lettie's bus trip to bury Uncle Osborn in Wyoming. She was carrying the urn with his ashes in a bowling ball bag, and the driver wanted to put the bag in the baggage compartment of the Greyhound bus…I digress, but that is another story for another time.

So here was the situation. The plane would land in Oakland at 5:15 p.m. and my car was in extended stay parking in Sacramento. I decided I should check with my husband. Maybe I could talk him into driving to Oakland to pick me up; it would just be a three or four hour round trip for him. Tomorrow I'd think of some way to get to the airport in Sacramento to pick up my car.

I called him from the baggage area and the conversation went something like this.

"Hi, Honey," with a conspiring little chuckle, "Guess what just happened?

"I have no idea," he answered sounding resigned, "but imagine you're about to tell me."

Not a good sign. "I'm in Oakland Airport, but my car is parked in Sacramento. What do you think we should do?" Did you notice how I made it our problem? I'm pretty shrewd with this reverse psychology stuff.

There was a very short pause. As I waited for his response I could hear Jeopardy in the background and then, "I'm going to watch the six o'clock news and I hope you have a good trip."

I sighed, so much for reverse psychology.

I'll Never Forget You

1937-2006

My daughter Karon, who lives in Tacoma, Washington, brought me the clipping from the newspaper when she came to visit in late March. An old classmate and neighbor of mine, from Whidbey Island had passed away. Whenever I hear someone I once knew, in a different time and place, dying, it brings a tug to my heart and memories come rushing back. You would think at my age I would be used to it, but each time I am a little saddened. Often the person is about my age and it's hard to believe I won't see them again. I still think of myself as in the prime of life and feel regret that another's life is cut so short. When it is my time I will be unprepared for I haven't done everything that I have set out to do. The news of my old friend's passing caught me by surprise, as I had been thinking of him lately and hoped to visit with him and his wife this next summer.

I first met Jack in the third grade at Langley Grade School. Even then, Jack was considered a leader, the class president. All through grade school he was a good student and very athletic. I think his favorite sport at that time was baseball. He was the pitcher, of course, and a home run king; the right fielder would move into deep backfield when he came up to bat. At home we often played "work-up" as it was difficult, in our small community, to get enough players for teams. We would dread the time Jack became the batter. It was almost impossible to put him out, and we would spend the rest of the game chasing his home runs. He approached his studies as he did sports...seriously.

Jack grew up with his family, overlooking Saratoga Beach, in a rough wood house that his father had built years before. His father was a commercial fisherman and the family lived close to the sea. Jack was the first son with two older sisters and a younger brother George. Many times my brother and I spent the day on the Metcalf's stationary raft, a couple hundred feet off shore, fishing for flounders and other bottom fish. The raft had a large submerged bait box and we were free to help ourselves, pretty sure that we would catch our dinner. The good fishing was what drew us there, but I secretly hoped that Jack would come out and join us.

The summer before we were to start high school, I got a job picking strawberries for Arnie Hoe, a local farmer, and was pleasantly surprised to find Jack and his brother among the crew. I was a pretty fast berry picker, but Jack set the bar even higher. We began an undeclared contest, to see who picked the most berries each day. The spirit of competition paid off, as I made more money that year than any previous year.

I often tell people that Jack was my school sweetheart during the fourth and again in the eighth grade. I never realized Jack was aware of my secret crush until 1994, when he reminded me of the first love letter I ever wrote. We attended the same grade school and occasionally attended social events in the community. For the most part the Metcalf family stayed close to their home in Saratoga, and unfortunately, we didn't see much of each other outside of school.

By the time we were in the eighth grade, it was evident that Jack was destined for a great future. From then on, he was captain of the football team, an outstanding baseball pitcher and a natural leader of his classmates. High school brought about a move for my family and although we lived within twenty miles of each other, we attended different schools. I saw little of him over the ensuing years, heard he was off to college and dating his high school sweetheart, Norma, whom he later married.

During WWII rumor had it that the Metcalf family (father) was a Socialist and very outspoken on political issues. This family interest in political issues marked the beginning of a long and successful career in local, state and national law making for Jack, which spanned over forty years. Once while visiting Olympia, the state capital of Washington State, I saw his name on the state senator rooster. It was nice to know that indeed, Jack had lived up to his promise.

Planning a visit to the northwest in 1994, my husband and I were looking at a tour book that featured Bed and Breakfast accommodations. We came across an ad for the Log Castle, owned and operated by Jack and Norma Metcalf. We spent several days as guests and enjoyed catching up on the past. It was at breakfast one morning, reminiscing and laughing about grade school, that Jack brought up "the letter." For over fifty years, I hadn't thought about the note I'd written him on the last day of fourth grade. "Oh my gosh, what ever did I say?" Jack smiled and told how he'd found the note under his binder as he was gathering his books to leave for the final time.

"Dear Jack," it started. "I'll see you next year. I won't forget you over the summer. Love, Mary Chase."

Although he had a long and notable career in state legislator, and was at the age when most people are ready to sit back and enjoy retirement, Jack successfully ran for Congress, and spent the next six years in D.C. I read a quirky article about one of his efforts to cut government spending in the Readers Digest. What it really said was that Jack could not be compromised when he believed he was right, even when it was an unpopular decision. I was in D.C. on AARP business and was staying at the Hyatt Hotel, near the Capitol, the evening Senator Dole was nominated as the Republican candidate for president. Congressmen and delegates were celebrating at the same hotel. By chance Jack and I shared the same elevator and a quick hello, promising more at a later time. Jack served his constituents and his country well.

It was the last time I actually saw Jack, but I heard he had retired, choosing not to run a fourth term. He returned to his family and beloved home at Saratoga on Whidbey Island in 2000. While my husband and I thought about a leisurely visit to the northwest sometime that summer, we talked about stopping in and perhaps staying at the Log Castle once again. Jack was a good and honest man, beloved or sometimes hated, but never ignored, by all who knew him.

I have always been able to recognize potential for greatness. In 1936, I may have been one of the first to realize that Jack was a little cut above his classmates. I wasn't at all surprised that he achieved so much. His philosophy and approach to life remained the simple fisherman's son I knew in our youth. He's gone now, but Jack, I won't ever forget you.

A Time for Courage

1994

A few weeks ago I happened upon a short sidebar in my local newspaper that caught my attention. The headline read: "Man unconscious after Disney World ride; dies." I went on to read: "ORLANDO, FLA--A 44-year old man died Tuesday after riding a roller coaster at Walt Disney World that simulates a runaway ride through the Himalayas, authorities said. Jeffery Reed, of Navarre, Fla., was pulled unresponsive from the ride, given CPR and pronounced dead at a local hospital. He had no visible signs of injury."

The article reminded me of a few years ago when I took two of my granddaughters, eight and six, to Disneyland, in Anaheim, on a long planned vacation. Cousins, Rachael and Christina, had talked of nothing else for the last week. We checked into the Disneyland Hotel where the girls enjoyed the swimming pool and seeing the Disney characters that frequented the restaurants and the hotel lobby. The next morning we visited the amusement park where we spent the day standing in line at the various rides, sang along with the bears at "It's a Small World," and ate a lot of junk food. The girls posed with Snow White as I took their picture. It was a typical day for 6 and 8 year olds, when finally exhausted, we found ourselves in line for the last ride of the day. As we stood waiting for our turn, I felt Christina pulling on my sleeve.

"What is it, honey?" I asked as the line moved closer to the gate.

"Grandma, it's a roller coaster," she whispered. "I don't want to go!" her eyes had a wild look and she was pulling me away from the line where Rachael waited.

I looked up at the monster rails and saw that she was right. Now, next to public speaking, riding on a roller coaster is my worst nightmare. I become faint just watching others terrified and screaming, clinging to the rail car as it hurls through space. It is out of the realm of my understanding why anyone would choose to ride on one; much less think it was fun. Rachael, on the other hand, thrived on the feeling of terror and was looking eagerly to board the car.

"Please Grandma," she begged. "Let's leave old sissy Christina here." Then as she saw my face, she continued. "Or, you can make her come with us."

Christina was near tears and I could feel her shaking. "I won't leave you here, Chris, and I won't make you go up in something that you don't want to."

Rachael, not one to give up easily, began negotiating again. "Christina can shut her eyes and we can put her in the middle. That way I'll be able to hang on to her." She kept edging us closer to the entrance.

I needed to take charge. "Now it's settled, I can't leave Christina in this crowd alone, and I promised your mother I wouldn't let you go on any rides by yourself.

Rachael looked at her whimpering cousin with disgust, and then turned her big brown eyes on me. I could see the wheels turning. Quickly I cut her off, "We need to get back to the hotel soon so you girls can go swimming before bedtime." I thought I had her for a moment, but there was more to come.

Head high, looking directly at me she asked point blank, "Are you afraid, Grandma?"

I had gone as far as I could with putting all the blame on Christina. It was confession time. "I'm deathly afraid, Rachael; I just can't do it." I paused briefly, and then with all the authority I could muster, I continued, "We are not going on that roller coaster."

She looked at me with concern. When she was satisfied that she had my full attention, she spoke with utter seriousness, "Grandma, you really need to ride that roller coaster; you need to face your fears now, or you will go through the rest of your life being afraid of riding a roller coaster." Ah, the wisdom of the young, I thought as I guided the girls back to the hotel.

Thinking about that day, I went back to the newspaper to finish reading the article. "Authorities are investigating whether Reed had a previous medical condition; an autopsy is planned. Inspectors found that the ride was working properly, but Disney kept it closed for further review. The ride made its debut in 2006 and featured an 80-foot drop."

An 80-foot drop; no wonder he died! I scanned the article again, yep, there it was, just as I fully expected; "It is believed that Jeffery Reed was accompanied on the ride by his 9 year old niece."

Neighborhood Watch

2008

It was my husband who first brought Jack to my attention. "Here's one I haven't noticed before," George said, gazing out the window. I realized that he was not referring to the letter he was trying to write, but focused on a lone jogger. A whole new world had opened up to my husband when he moved his computer worksite over near the window that faced the front of our home. The house is on the north side of a quiet meandering street with almost no through traffic. Residents on Panorama Drive live behind closed doors. Backyards sport pools for casual entertainment so it's rare to see your neighbors, except leaving or pulling into their garages.

It wasn't until George repositioned himself that we realized that dozens of walking/jogging enthusiasts pass this way daily. From his vantage point at the window he witnessed a kaleidoscope of activity. Nearly a recluse, due to health and design, my husband was enjoying a new experience. Without leaving his armchair he became engaged in other people's lives. For the last year he had followed the saga of a man and a woman who initially could barely waddle around the block. George watched fascinated, as the couple walked, then jogged day after day, following their progress with grudging admiration.

"Here he is again. Come look. Do you know this fellow?" He asked a few days later.

I moved to the window, but by that time I just caught a glimpse of the jogger's backside as he disappeared around the turn in the street. "What's so special about him?" I wanted to know.

"I don't know-- he's sort of all over the place. Maybe he's just starting to jog and hasn't gotten his stride yet."

I think I owe it to you, the reader, to let you in on a little quirk of mine. For years I have had this compulsion to spin a story, in my mind, around a person who I really don't know, having just met or noticed him or her at an event. Never mind that there may be no foundation or truth in what I fabricate, it becomes real to me. Later, I'm often astounded when I learn that I was completely off track

A few days after George pointed out the new runner on our street I spotted him jogging as I drove to the store. I noticed that he jogged slightly pigeon toed, which accounted for George's description of him "being all over the place." He appeared to have a soulful expression, and his dark hair fell over his forehead and with that much information my imagination took over. "His name is Jack and he recently broke up with his wife or maybe it was his live-in girlfriend." I informed George as he helped me unload the groceries.

"Who broke up with his wife?"

"The new jogger you saw the other day. His name is Jack, and he just moved to Riverbank after a very rough divorce. I think he might sell real estate."

George looked at me curiously "You were only gone 15 minutes, where did you get all this information?"

I had a feeling that he wasn't going to believe me as I continued. "I saw him jogging over on the next street, and I could just tell by looking at him."

"You didn't talk to him, you just made all this up?" He shook his head and walked back to the TV. We've been married over 40 years and he has learned to pick his battles.

In the following weeks I noticed Jack often as his jogging improved, but continued to worry about him. I hoped he would find a new woman to fill his life. I've always been a hopeless romantic.

One day I went out to get the mail and there was Jack on my lawn trying to catch a lively black lab pup that was bouncing around him in figure eights. The pup thought it was all a game and wiggled his whole body in delight as Jack made a futile lunge for him. Jack looked up and the dog followed his gaze as I came out the front door. "Your dog seems to have gotten out." Jack offered as an explanation for being on my lawn.

"That's not my dog." I assured him.

"Well it came out from around your house."

"But it's not my dog."

Jack looked down at the dog, which was now leaning against his bare leg with an expectant look on his face, and then back at me. I steeled myself as I heard the distress in his voice as he tried once again: "Do you know who owns this dog?"

They looked so right for each other that I made a quick decision. "It seems you got yourself a friend, and I think you ought to call him Barney," I told him as I headed up the steps. As I entered the house, I had to smile as Barney jumped up and nearly knocked Jack over. I didn't watch them leave, I knew Jack would do the right thing.

"I feel better." I told George at dinner that evening. "Jack's got himself a dog. He won't be so lonesome now."

Three weeks later George called me to the window and together we watched Jack jog by with Barney. Jack struggled to keep his balance as Barney tangled the two of them in his new leash. I sighed, "I hope they go to obedience school together soon."

By summer Jack and Barney, now nearly full grown, were a familiar sight. Later Jack rode by on his bicycle with Barney proudly at his side. At the end of summer I happened to see Jack and Barney walk by, accompanied by a woman. George grunted when I told him that Jack had taken Barney over to the dog park and they had met a pretty woman there with her yellow lab. *Looks like there was going to be wedding bells soon,* I congratulated myself on my fine matchmaking and was so pleased that *Jack had a new wife and a faithful dog. Such a happy ending!* Or so I thought.

Things never go exactly as one plans. I attend an evening writing group and we were to meet one Thursday at my house. We are always trying to recruit new members, so I was quite pleased when on Tuesday, before our meeting, I was given the phone number of a woman who was interested in joining the group. I called her and discovered that she lived only a block away. We exchanged information about our writing and she told me she had written a book and was trying to get it published. I explained that I was into my memoirs and currently concentrating on short stories—most recently a Trilogy called *Neighborhood Watch*.

On Thursday, before the meeting, I was in a rush. In my haste, when I tried to print my story "*JACK,*" the paper jammed and I couldn't get it out.

I struggled with it for about five minutes, succeeding only in shredding the bottom of the page. *The heck with it,* I decided. *I won't read tonight. I'll just listen and critique the others.*

The evening was a great success, with good writing and a lot of lively discussion. The new member, Karen, appeared to enjoy herself and I felt sure she would be coming back. She told the group that she had seen the ad about our writing group last April in the paper, and it had been on her refrigerator ever since. As I walked her to the door we chatted and she wanted to know a little more about "Neighborhood Watch."

I explained that I'm writing about life as seen from my office window. I plan to have three separate short stories and I'd finished the first one. "I'm calling the first one *Jack.* It's a story about a man I had noticed jogging past our house several years ago, and how his finding a dog had changed his life."

She looked at me carefully and said, "My husband has a dog, and you might have noticed him jogging with his black lab?" She paused waiting for me to say something, and then when I remained speechless she continued, "In fact when I told him I was coming over here, he made a comment, something to the affect, that he wondered if the meeting tonight was at the home of the lady that pushed Sadie, that's his dog, off on him." She chuckled, "he really loves that dog."

"Sadie?" I asked incredulously. "Barney is a girl?" It's funny how the mind works in times of stress. Thinking back quickly over my story, I asked myself, *could it possibly be? Of course, I 'm not known as "Old Foot In Her Mouth," for nothing.* What are the odds? Was it just a coincidence? Or was it that my guardian angel knew exactly what she was doing when she jammed my printer?

Jumping to Conclusions

2008

"I see we are getting new neighbors." George announced coming out of the office. "The moving van just pulled up at Brad's house." Brad had been gone for three or four years and there had been a series of renters, but "Brad's house" was how we always referred to the house across the street. Ever since George moved his computer near the window he liked to report on the happenings he witnessed. He left it up to me to fill in the details.

"Do they have children?" I asked, always curious about new neighbors.

"I only saw the moving van," he replied as he took his second cup of coffee out on the patio.

While I checked out the large orange and white U-Haul truck, a red Nissan came around the corner and parked behind it. An attractive blonde got out of the car and walked up to the cab of the truck. She stood talking to the driver, gesturing toward the driveway. Just then my phone rang and I didn't think about our new neighbors again until late in the afternoon when I left to go to the library.

I waved at the small group gathered in the open garage of Brad's house. *Probably taking a well-deserved break*, I thought to myself. When I returned the garage door was closed, and the U-Haul truck was nowhere to be seen.

"I noticed a couple of kid's bikes," I told George as I set my load of books on the kitchen counter.

"Who has a couple of kids?" George asked off handedly as he dug through my bag of books from the library, finally selecting a large nonfiction book about WWII.

"I think our new neighbors do." I had more information. "I saw them taking a break in the garage as I went to the library." I paused, and then continued carefully, "I'm not sure but I think they are a bi-racial family. At least half the people I saw moving furniture are black."

"That'll be a first around here. Are you sure?"

"I saw what I saw. Look for yourself."

"I'll take your word for it." George grunted as he open the book he had chosen and settled into his favorite chair. I wouldn't hear much from him for the next day or so while he relived his past as a paratrooper in the South Pacific.

I thought about the new family as I went about making one of my specialties; chicken enchilada casserole. I had decided to make two of them; one for our dinner and one for the family moving in. While the chicken cooked I thought how nice it would be to have young children across the street once again. We had specifically chosen our new home when we retired, not only for the house we loved, but also for the fact that the neighborhood was multi-generational.

I had told George that our new neighbors were bi-racial, based on noting that the woman who seemed to be in charge was a blonde with fair skin coloring and the man driving the U-Haul was definitely African-American. The rest of the movers were mostly black. As usual I had filled in the blanks from my imagination. I wondered how I really felt about living next door to an African American family. I had always prided myself on being open-minded and had worked with many minorities, but had never lived in an integrated community.

As a child I grew up on Whidbey Island and was 14 years old before I remember seeing my first black person. My parents were concerned about anyone and everyone different from themselves. My father, in particular, used slang racial names when talking about most minorities. I grew up hearing neighbors referred to as Wops, Dagos, Niggers, Spicks, Krauts, and Japs, and of course, the money grabbing Jews.

Although my father referred to others by nationality I never saw or heard him be disrespectful to their face. He worked side-by-side with people of all races, and got along well, but when Papa spoke about them he invariably referenced his story with a racial or slang name. A co-worker was referred to as "Deafy." My father was of first generation Swedish descent and I think he got a surprise when we first moved to Whidbey Island into a hotbed of Norwegians. All of a sudden we were the minority. My brother came home from school and proclaimed that Swedes were 'nothing but Norwegian with their brains knocked out!" When I entered high school and became aware of the real world I started challenging my parents' beliefs, and we had many heated discussions. My mother tried to explain that she really wasn't prejudice, but what she believed was really the truth and attempted to illustrate her points.

There are all kinds of prejudices. My experiences were limited to growing up in a rural all-white community where your father's occupation, the house you lived in, how smart you were in school, how good your were in sports, and your looks helped or hindered your—actually determined where you fit in the social scale. I was sure if only I had curls like Shirley Temple and could tap dance I would be much more popular.

As an adult and raising my own children I preached tolerance and acceptance, and truly believed in fairness to all. Through my work and volunteering for AARP I have had numerous opportunities to get to know people of all religions, color and backgrounds. In the last 12 years I worked along side many blacks and was conscious that I finally could use the old saying "I'm not prejudiced, some of my best friends are black."

The next day I took my chicken enchiladas casserole, and welcomed the new family to Panorama Drive. The blond woman I had seen driving the Nissan introduced herself, and the small boy peeking around her legs as her youngest son, Jared. He appeared to be about eight years old and his large dark eyes glowed with curiosity. "You got any kids over there I can play with?"

"I'm afraid not, but sometimes my grandchildren come visit, and actually I have a grandson just about your size." I waved at the teenager shooting baskets at the side of the house. Teri thanked me for the casserole and we exchanged pleasantries as she walked me down the sidewalk.

In the following weeks I noticed her husband, and oldest son Geoff, working in the yard. Since Brad had moved, it had fallen in disarray. Shrubs and trees were overgrown and unsightly. During the long summer months the property changed from neglect to one of the best-kept and attractive yards on our block.

As the weeks passed, our relationship remained at the "hello and wave stage." I rarely saw the boys except when they were shooting baskets or coming or going to school.

Geoff surprised me one day by coming over and saying he was assigned community service through his school and volunteered to put out and return my trash cans each week. We got acquainted over some homemade chocolate chip cookies. I learned he wanted to go into the service when he graduated from high school in a couple years but his dad was set on his going to college first. He smiled when he told me about their disagreement. "After all," he explained, "my dad is an Army Recruiter. You'd think he would be proud if I went in the service." Geoff looked so earnest and so young. He reminded me of one of my own grandsons, at odds with his father.

Each neighborhood has its own rhythm. Panorama Drive, located off main streets and only two blocks long, was peaceful and had little through traffic. Kids often played catch in the street and for the most part cars that went by belonged there. People jogged and walked the area at all times of day and evening, a safe and secure neighborhood. In all, we felt so secure that we never have bothered to organize an official Neighborhood Watch Team.

The months passed, and life remained good on Panorama Drive. Friendly neighbors and I never gave it another thought about any possible problems until a small incident happen that jarred my concept of my own values.

One Sunday a friend, Jo, picked me up and after church we had a late brunch together at a local restaurant. She pulled in front of my home and we sat making plans for a date later in the week. I was sitting sideways and out of the corner of my eye I noticed an old black car traveling faster than normal, headed our way. As it came up the street I could see that the passenger's side door was crumpled and the car looked out of place.

The old car slowed and made a wide U-turn directly in front of where we sat. All that registered was a sea of laughing black faces and a head or two of cornrows. From the time I first spotted the car until it pulled to the opposite curb, only a few seconds had passed and my riveting thought was, "What is that car doing on my street?"

"What's the matter?" Jo wanted to know.

My mind was racing, wondering what a car full of black youths was doing across the street from my home. I watched in silence as a tall teenager climbed out of the back seat, and walked across my neighbor's lawn.

Catcalls and whistle followed him around to the side of the house as the beat-up car pulled out and disappeared down the block.

It wasn't until I saw him pick up a basketball and neatly shoot it through the hoop tacked on the garage door did I realize it was Geoff, who liked my chocolate chip cookies and took out my trash cans. The truth about myself hit me hard.

Haste Makes Waste

2009

I awoke Monday morning with a nagging feeling that there was something that needed to be done today. Monday morning, April 13th and it suddenly came to me with a jolt. I had procrastinated long enough. Like it or not, it was only two days until final filing date; it was H & R Block time; but then, what's the rush, right?

Over my second cup of coffee I called for an appointment, thinking that it would be a day or so before I could get in. To my surprise I was given an appointment for that very afternoon at 2:00 p.m. I spent the morning going over everything in my Income Tax folder and filling out the work sheet. As usual, several year-end reports from my mutual funds were not in the folder and I had to scramble around looking for them. Time was pressing.

It was soon evident I had not paid enough withholding tax during the year and consequently I would have to send additional funds to both the IRS and the State Franchise Board. I located my checkbook and looked to be sure I had plenty of blank checks. "Good thinking!" I congratulated myself staring at the lone blank check. I grabbed a new book and gathered up my work sheet and the folder with all the necessary receipts.

Anita, at H & R Block, has done my taxes for the past five years so she knows more about my finances than I do. She has all my tax history in her computer system and over the years we have become friendly. "Calling it pretty close this year aren't you. Mary?"

"I don't know where the time goes, but here I am."

I watch fearfully as she entered the information and I didn't like the frown on her face. "I see you didn't take my advice about increasing your estimated taxes," she scolded.

"I thought my huge medical bills this year would make up for it," I explained. "Doesn't work that way. You only get a percentage of out-of-pocket costs."

The good feeling of getting a tough job out of the way was being replaced with dread. I could tell this year was going to be a zinger. I promised myself, as I do each April, that next year would be different. "I'll increase the monthly deductible and keep better records of everything. None of this last minute rush," I swore.

"Well Mary, you didn't do too badly with the state but here's what you owe the IRS."

I swallowed several times and bit my lip. There was nothing to do, except to pay up. I wrote a check to H & R for doing my taxes on the last blank check. I then dug out the new book and wrote two checks to the IRS, one covering what I owed for the year 2008 and the first estimated taxes for 2009. I did the same for the Franchise Tax Board.

"Now don't you feel better, getting this taken care of?" It was easy for Anita to say. In reality, even though I owed much more than I had thought, I did feel like a great weight had been lifted.

During the next week I wrote a few local checks, including my housekeeper. I was surprised when she appeared on my doorstep a few days later. "Mary," she began, waving some papers in my face, "your check was no good. My bank charged me $12.00 for the bad check."

I couldn't believe it. "I don't know how that happened, there's plenty in my checking account."

"They said you don't have an account and they charged me $12.00. See!" as she thrust the offending bank statement at me. I looked closely at the returned check and it took a few seconds to register. I had mistakenly used a new checkbook from a joint account that I had closed a year ago when my husband died. I wrote her a new check on my current account and added the $12.00 that her bank had charged her. She left happy.

Remember how good I was feeling after taking care of having my taxes done? Life is never simple; try reaching the IRS and explaining how you accidentally used checks on an account that has been closed for a year.

I phoned my daughter, "If you call and can't reach me, you might try the federal prison. I really did it this time." I paused for dramatic effect, and then I confessed, "I paid my income taxes with hot checks."

Incident at Deception Pass

July 2009

The sun was directly overhead and the in-coming waves rolled up the rocky shore. A few boats could be seen entering the narrow passage on their way to the open waters of *The Straits-Of-San-De-Fuca*. Karen and her friend climbed down the steep path and moved up the beach in search of agates and shells. I had declined their invitation to join them and waited on a park bench enjoying the spectacular view.

At water's edge stood a large rock formation that was a beacon for most of the tourists as they spilled out of their vehicles and ran across the rocky beach. It demanded to be climbed and explored, and was a natural background for picture taking. From where I waited I had a front row seat to all the activity.

"People watching" has always been a favorite past time, so I enjoyed basking in the warm sunshine while people came and went. I have a theory that if you watch a crowd long enough you will eventually witness all of human behavior. I became engrossed in noticing new arrivals climb their way down the rough path and made a mental note of the men who started down and then turned to assist their female companion. Those who reached back and helped their companion received a mental a gold star.

I spied two beautiful long-legged teen-aged girls walking towards the water. They stopped half way and stood laughing, looking back at the parking lot. A golden boy, who looked about fourteen, came staggering towards them with another young girl on his back. All four were obviously brother and sisters. With their long blonde hair whipping in the sea breeze, laughing faces, and designer beach wear, the entire scene could have been taken right out of a movie set. I thought perhaps that I was about to witness a publicity shoot of the rich and famous frolicking on the beach.

The teens made straight for the rock and an older woman, whom I assumed was their mother, moved into my line of vision. She had her predictable camera ready. The father was on his cell and stood apart but eventually joined them at the top of the rock. Even during the group posing and the picture taking he never put the phone down, nor did I see him interact with any of them. The mother and her children were laughing and ignoring the man. Finally the entire group climbed down and moved to the water's edge and stood pointing and talking. The father was turned away from his family and deep in his phone conversation.

I waited for him to finish and to join his family, but he was completely engrossed, and oblivious to what was going on around him. I silently stewed as I watched the drama unfold. The woman and her teenagers were laughing and enjoying the moment; the man was outside the family, not emotionally connected. I wanted to yell at him. I felt I should somehow make him understand how fast time goes and these wonderful few moments will not happen again. I sighed and remembered what my husband had often told me that it wasn't up to me to save the world.

But soon, in a trance like state, I felt myself climb down the steep path and move up the beach until I was facing the man with the phone. I raised my voice to be heard over lapping of the waves. "For God's sake put the phone away!" He frowned and moved aside, probably thinking I was yelling at someone else. "You; I'm talking to you. Put the phone down and enjoy your family." By this time I'm nearly in his face. He looked around startled, and in retrospect, I'm sure he thought that he had met up with a crazy woman.

"Lady, I don't know what your problem is but I'm on a very important call." He turned away from me as I grabbed at the phone. "What are you, some sort of nut?" As we struggled for the phone, I tripped and fell into the sand. I became aware for the first time that we now had an audience watching with varying degrees of curiosity. Suddenly my daughter appeared demanding to know what was going on.

I sat sprawled awkwardly on the wet sand. "Why did you push my mother down?" Karen demanded to know. "What happened here? Mare, are you hurt? Do I need to call the police?"

"I didn't mean to knock her down. She was yelling at me and trying to grab my phone." He looked confused and embarrassed. "I'm on an important phone call that means a lot of money, and I don't even know where she came from."

"That's no reason to knock an 80-year-old woman down." Karen looked ready to take him on herself so I needed to put a stop to this nonsense immediately.

"It was an accident Karen, he was just trying to protect what is his and I slipped. I'm not hurt. And he's right, it is my fault and absolutely none of my business. I just couldn't stand seeing him on the phone missing everything."

"Well…"she hesitated, not sure just what she should do next, "if you're sure you're not hurt. Here, let me help you up."

I brushed the seat of my pants off and turned once more to the man. "I apologize for yelling at you and trying to grab your phone."

"That's okay." He muttered. "It really is an important call and I need to get back to it; they are probably wondering what is going on."

"Well just remember, when you are old and you want to spend time with your grown children they probably will be too busy making money to spend time with you." I always need to have the last word, even when I'm wrong.

"Hey Mare, taking a little snooze in the sun?" I shook my head surprised at her question. Slightly confused I looked around unable to spot the man with the phone.

"No, of course not, I just…" I quickly retorted. Suddenly understanding my *Walter Mitty* experience I laughed and confessed, "I guess I did drop off for a few minutes."

Love At First Sight

2009

I felt almost lightheaded as I dialed my son's cell phone. I knew he was going to be pleased with my news. He and I had been through so much grief together these past two years and now there was a light at the end of the tunnel. As his phone rang and I waited for him to pick up I visualized him checking the caller ID and I could almost hear him mumbling to himself. "What now? What more can go wrong?"

Finally on the fifth and last ring before the call would cut to voice mail he answered, his voice filled with caution. "Hi, what's up?"

"Oh Pat, I'm so glad to catch you. I've got some wonderful news and I want you to be the first to hear it."

"You got some good news?" He sounded kind of grumpy, not that I could blame him after the last month.

"Pat, I think I'm in love. His name is Jeremy and if he's not married I think I'll marry him…well maybe not marry him. But this is the one, I know and I want you to meet him and see what you think"

I could hear Pat give a big sigh. "Wait a minute, you've already found a new one? I can't believe it, especially after Eddie. I never thought you would try again. My gosh, Mom, after everything Eddie put you through I can't believe that you are over all of that!"

I really couldn't blame Pat for being cynical, and getting him back over here was not as easy as I'd hoped. "Pat, I want this to be the right decision. I think it is, but since you have been with me from the beginning on this I was hoping that you could come over and meet Jeremy and see what you think."

"What is this Mom, number four since Dad died?"

"Actually, the first two were when your dad was still alive; that is, Eric first and then six months later it was Terry. Eric was a complete disaster and then I really thought, or at least hoped that Terry would take care of things. I was almost sick when I found out that Terry couldn't be trusted. It didn't take me long to realize that he never kept his word. As you know he would promise to see me at a certain time, then he wouldn't show, no phone call and no excuse when he finally waltzed in."

"What about Eddie. Are you completely through with him?"

"Absolutely, I got a lawyer and the papers have been filed. My lawyer says it is an open and shut case and with you testifying there shouldn't be any problems. The only thing is I don't have a court date yet. Seems there is a big backlog and since it is not life threatening it might be a while before we go to court. Now I've met Jeremy and I want to get on with my life. Say you will come over."

"I don't know if I want to get involved again. I didn't help you with Eddie." I waited while he thought about his busy schedule and finally, "Where did you say you found this guy? Jeremy, is it?"

"Dave gave me his telephone number." I realized that Pat didn't know who Dave was so I beat him to his next question. "Dave is my furnace man. We've had him for years. Every fall I call him and he comes by to check the flue and light my pilot light on my gas insert. Anyway, we got talking while he was here and I told him my troubles with Eric, Terry and now Eddie. Then with out my even asking, he told me he had the perfect guy for me. Before he left he called Jeremy and introduced us over the phone." I waited for Pat to say something but was greeted only with silence, so I continued. "He came over that night and we just hit it off. Now he is coming back in the morning and that's why I want you here."

"I sure hope you are not jumping from the frying pan into the fire. I'll be over, don't do anything rash 'til I get there."

"Well Pat, I'm ready to take the next step and you know I said that if I could ever find an honest plumber I'd marry him."

Open Letter To Lena

February 2009

My Dear Grandma Lena,

I am to write a letter of tribute, as a class assignment, to someone whom I admire. I mentally went through the long list of wonderful and exciting people who I have been privileged to know in my lifetime and am surprised how many deserve this distinction.

However, I'm to write but one letter. As I struggled with choosing whom I should honor, you came to mind and are the obvious choice.

I'm older today than you were when you passed on. It seems that I spent an entire lifetime rarely giving you a thought until a few years ago. In 1996 while visiting New York City, I had an opportunity to explore Ellis Island where you spent your first five days in America. I had armed myself with the few facts I had about your arrival in United States, from your native Sweden in 1880. What a bleak welcome that must have been and I wonder what you could have been thinking. Were you excited and looking forward to a new life; or were you frightened to find your self in a strange country where you could barely speak the language?

How courageous you must have been to travel so far knowing only that you were to work for a family somewhere in the Wyoming Territory as an indentured servant. What were your thoughts as you crossed thousands of wilderness miles by rail knowing you would never see your native homeland again?

One hundred and twenty-seven years ago you married Lendell Chase, who eventually became my grandfather. I can't imagine a more unlikely pair…a small pretty immigrant from Karap Venge, Sweden, and a cocky Canadian masquerading as a Frontier Vigilante.

Grandmother Lena Nelsen Chase

I don't believe I ever heard how you and my grandfather met, but I have a vague recollection of being told that he paid your passage debt to the Hughes family. I realize that times were different then but I need to ask, how did that make you feel? Were you grateful or did you feel like a piece of livestock being sold to the highest bidder? Oh Grandma, I'm so sorry.

Lendell Chase was not an attractive man. He was short, and born with a cleft palette, which made his speech difficult to understand, and one eye was cocked. I'm sure that his short fuse was even more disturbing to your gentle nature. He was permanently crippled from an accident in 1910 while driving a twenty-mule team and wagon, loaded with ore, down a mountainside.

According to our family history you and Lendell were married in 1882 and you soon started your family. Three boys and one girl were born in the next seven years, while you were living in Nebraska. Your family then moved to Cornish, New Hampshire, where eventually another son was born. Finally in 1898, still living in New Hampshire, now 38 years old, you became pregnant for the final time.

I heard the story of Lynn and Letty's birth many times. You had hoped that Lewis, now nearly four years of age was going to be your last child. This pregnancy was more difficult than the others and you spent several weeks in bed prior to delivery. I was told that at birth, the girl baby was born first and then Lynn, the smaller of the two. At delivery he was limp and not breathing on his own. Supposedly the doctor had *"tossed him aside and worked to save the girl twin."* You were said to have demanded someone hand you the boy baby and somehow you were able to revive him. If this is an accurate account I owe you a special thanks, for obviously I wouldn't be writing this letter if he had died at birth. Was he really so small that the first few days he was bedded in a cigar box? That's small! Could it have been a shoebox? I hate to question a family tale, but I have no one else to ask.

That you favored your youngest son was taken for granted among the family. According to his twin Letty, Lynn was sickly as a child and required a great deal of attention from you. In later years she let everyone know that *"she felt that she never had a mother."*

My dad and twin sister, Letty, 1905

Always restless and looking for a better life, Lendell moved your family back to Wyoming around 1900 and went into freighting business. He secured a twenty--mule team and large wagons and began hauling supplies to the oil fields. The twins started the first grade in Saratoga. Were you content with your family? I've seen pictures of you at home on the prairie. Did you long to speak with others in your native tongue or see your homeland once again? It must have been a difficult and perhaps lonely existence for you.

In 1911, while living in Casper, Wyoming Grandpa was engaged in hauling supplies to the mines and bringing ore down the mountain. On his return trip, loaded with ore, the team spooked and he attempted to stop the run-a-way wagon. His leg was broken in several places. The doctor set the bone and hung it with weights on a pulley. It was a slow and painful method to try to keep the bone in alignment so it could heal.

Months later exhausted from caring for your injured husband, who was a difficult and angry patient, you needed time out. Your four oldest children were grown and on their own, so with only Lewis and the twins you moved in with friends who lived in Saratoga, California, to get your strength back. Eventually Grandpa Lendell settled in Livingston, California, and built a nice house to entice you back. I love it that you took your time before you joined him there in 1915. The twins were now 17 and Letty soon married and moved on to her own life, leaving Lynn the only child at home.

New Home 1915

You were disappointed when Lynn married in 1921 after a very brief courtship in Yosemite. He brought Gladys to Livingston soon after they married to start their life together. Were you upset that your 'baby" married or was there something about her that you didn't like? I always felt that she wasn't really accepted by the Chase Family. Was it that she was a "modern woman" and failed to defer to her husband, or that her hair was cut short and she smoked in public? I often wondered if it was just because you were jealous because Lynn, my Papa, adored his wife.

Lendell died in 1926, a year before I was born. Mama described the funeral to me when I asked about him. She told me that he had been a tyrant and a wretched man. However, Papa is said to have cried when he was buried, but that your eyes were dry. You were only 67 years old and now a widow.

There is a mystic haze surrounding my memories of you. I can see you dressed always in long black skirts with many petticoats. I was told that as winter approached you would begin adding petticoat for warmth, a forerunner of the layering we do now. Then as spring and the warm weather began you would start removing them. You wore high-top black shoes and shawls topped your shoulders. Your lovely hair, blonde in your youth, was silver by the time we met, and was never cut. I remember you wore it braided and wound loosely around your head, giving you a regal look. You were very small; however, you carried your self so ramrod straight I thought you were much taller than you really were. With your high cheekbones and chiseled features you were truly a beautiful woman.

My first eight years we lived only a short walk from your home in Livingston, California, so I should have many memories of times we spent together. However, Uncle Lewis, his wife and two children lived with you. I was jealous of Barbara Jean and Edgar and never felt that you were totally my grandmother. It wasn't until I started this letter to you that I remembered how you would sometimes take me aside and invite me into your bedroom. With an air of conspiracy you'd check the door to be sure that we were alone and ask me about school or my brothers. Then, as I shivered with anticipation you'd go into the dark recesses of your closet and bring out your secret box of chocolates. I could then choose one piece. You cautioned me not to *"tell"* the others. I remember feeling very special.

It was after my family had moved to Whidbey Island that you and I shared a bedroom for a short winter. We said our nightly prayers together kneeling on the bitter cold bare floor and I longed for the warm bed piled high with many quilts. I'd get through my "Now I lay me down…" in record time, but I had to wait for you to finish. You talked to God in your native tongue and seemed to go on and on. I shivered in my thin cotton nightgown.

Grandma Lena, 1936

Things kind of came to a head between you and Mama while you stayed with us. The problem seemed to center around the kitchen. Since then I've learned that there isn't a kitchen anywhere big enough for two strong willed women, who love the same man. In my heart I sided with Mama and I think everyone was a little relieved when you announced that you were returning to California to take care of Uncle Lewis and his two children. You told me you didn't want to leave me, but they didn't have a mother anymore. I thought you were leaving because it was too cold for you in Washington.

Papa loaded your trunk on the back of Lewis's old truck and you climbed inside the cab and pulled Edgar on your lap, settling in for the long journey. I never saw you again, and when I would think about you, I was glad that you were finally warm. In February, 1939, we received word that you had died. Soon your nice house in Livingston was sold and you left a tiny inheritance for each of your grandchildren.

There are so many things I will never learn about you. I often wish that you had waited for me to grow up and we could have become friends. It was only after I was grown and had children and grandchildren of my own that I realized what a brave and loving woman you were.

Hello Reality

2009

A few years ago I finally realized that I was actually old. I knew I had been moving in that direction for some time, but refused to embrace the truth. Others, those that loved me, noticed but for the most part avoided the obvious. One evening, while my husband was still here, we were walking to our car following an event at the State Theater when a carload of youths out looking for excitement sped by. Spying us, one young man stuck his head out the window and yelled in our direction. "Hey you...hey you ah, ah...you, you old people you!" It struck us as insanely funny at the time.

Now that I've admitted that I am indeed "old" I have come to the realization that being "old" is not funny. My biggest concern is loss of identity. Throughout my middle years I viewed myself positively. If asked, "Who are you?" it was easy to identify myself as a leader in the nursing field, a decision maker, wife and a mother. Along with that I would have added that I was healthy, friendly, honest and often funny.

My second major concern as I grew older was the loss of independence. I always thought I was perfectly capable of taking care of myself and as a caregiver of others. The thought of physical decline depresses me.

I have a natural tendency to put things off, and so it has been in planning how I would deal with getting old. It's called "procrastination" and I've had this problem all of my life. To be truthful, I knew, of course, that if I lived long enough I would eventually get old, I just didn't think that "eventually" would ever become "now." I didn't think it would happen when I was so young.

I have been retired from a satisfying career for many years. Originally the idea of retirement sounded wonderful, as my husband, long retired, was happily involved in Network Marketing. I, on the other hand, had no idea what I would do to fill the long hours. We, who procrastinate, wait for things to get real close before we do anything. A few months into this vagueness of retirement the phone rang one Thursday afternoon. It was my former CEO, Sandie Rogers. They wanted me back at work; the State of California could not get along without my expertise! Like honey to the bees, like a drug to an addict, the offer made my day. I promised to report back to work on Monday as a Nurse Consultant for the Department of Developmental Services (DDS).

This assignment as a Nurse Consultant kept me off the streets at night for five years until my Tax Accountant persuaded me that I was actually working for free and the only one to benefit financially was the IRS. It has been a slow process, letting go of a self-image that had grown over thirty-seven years. I was lucky for it was during this time I found volunteering for AARP as a way to engage in activities that were meaningful rewarding and involved with other people. I would be using many of the skills that I had learned in the past. It was a wonderful opportunity. I was so happy to find a home for my energy and commitment to others. Thinking differently about who I was and what I was doing was not as difficult as I imagined it would be. Moving on once again and each time I enter a new phase I left something of myself behind.

Over the years I've had the best: a successful career, a long marriage, rewarding volunteer experiences, friends and a warm relationship with my children. Now I am aware of my limitations and ultimately about mortality. I finally admit to myself that I will not enter any more jitterbug contests nor will I take that parachute jump I have been planning. It was to occur on my fortieth birthday but due to putting things off I just haven't gotten around to it yet and now I probably won't.

There has been significant change in my physical and mental capacities following a serious illness last year. Having to use a walker, followed by the use of a cane, has changed my relationship to everyone I meet. I hate it! At first I couldn't stand the offer of help from family or friends. I'm beginning to accept that limited ambulation is a permanent state. Writing this I realize there is a major change in my attitude towards being old.

Writing about the past for my memoirs is helping me to move ahead. I often stir up memories that fill me with laughter or occasionally yearning for the hectic days before my life completely changed. Those thoughts take me back to the teamwork that I developed with my co-workers and fellow volunteers. I've become fully engaged in Modesto Institute for Continued Learning (MICL) and in writing particularly. I have a whole new set of teammates, the Board of Directors and Committee Chairs and my peers in our writing group. I like this new voyage I'm on and I count on MICL to help me steer the course, fair weather or foul.